BLACK FALCON

CHEVY ALDEN

To David Wertz,
"Live Your Dreams"

TRI-PACER PRESS
PEMBROKE PINES, FLORIDA

All characters and events depicted in this novel are fictitious creations of the author. Any resemblance to real people, living or dead, or to real events is purely coincidental.

Published by:
TRI-PACER PRESS
P.O. Box 840111
Pembroke Pines, FL 33084

Copyright© 1986, 1988 by Richard Cook
Library of Congress Catalog Card Number: 88-50158
ISBN 0-9619991-5-2

All Rights Reserved. This book may not be reproduced in whole or in part by mimeograph or any other means without written permission from the publisher.

Printing History
First Printing: October 1988
Second Printing: March 1991
Third Printing: January 1996

Printed in the United States of America

ATTENTION: AVIATION & NAUTICAL GROUPS

Is your organization looking for a highly-motivated guest speaker to tell your members how they can write and publish their own air-sea books? Award-winning author Chevy Alden makes year-round guest appearances at aviation and nautical-related trade shows, conferences and association meetings. For detailed information, please write to: Alden Speaking Engagements, c/o Tri-Pacer Press, P. O. Box 840111, Pembroke Pines, Florida, 33084-2111.

ACKNOWLEDGMENTS

Special thanks go to *George Diamond, Ph.D.*, whose creative criticism and encouragement kept *BLACK FALCON* a viable project for seven long years.

Special thanks also go to my editor/copyeditor, *Beth Hagan,* whose exceptional faith in *BLACK FALCON* allowed her to take on such a difficult task.

Appreciated thanks go to: My wife, *Bonnie,* who endured many lonely nights while I wrote *BLACK FALCON.* My parents, *Morris* and *Sarina,* who put up with a lot of craziness from me over the years. *Jennifer P. Tucker,* who did a great job on *BLACK FALCON's* cover art. *Humberto (Tony) Miranda,* who provided me with the Spanish translations and slang for *BLACK FALCON. Molly Siobhan McGill,* who lent me her AX-12 electronic typewriter for the final rewrite of *BLACK FALCON.*

In memory of George Pagar, who taught me the meaning of freedom.

BLACK FALCON

"I reached my thirtieth...and 84/P-18/A, F.E.A."
r.c.

PROLOGUE

Early morning in mid-February

The gravel-faced captain maintained a firm grip on the Lodestar's control wheel as he hand flew the twin-engined aircraft just fifty feet above the Florida Straits. He was thinking about the rip-off, wondering if it would go down as planned, wondering if he'd have enough guts to pull the trigger of his .357 Magnum. He had never killed a man before. Would it be the same as killing a deer? He wondered a bit more, then put his mind back on flying the airplane.

After scanning the panel, the captain turned his gaze out the windshield. A full moon hung low above the horizon as it made its nightly descent against the western sky. Below, the waves' crests sparkled in the moon's effervescence, creating an eerie, yet tranquilizing feeling for the pilot.

The Lodestar's copilot, meanwhile, was paying no particular attention to nature's artistry, although he, too, was looking out the aircraft's windshield. His eyes were busy darting around, searching in the distant early morning darkness for a certain man-made landmark. He was sure his navigational calculations were correct. Or were they? Maybe he had figured the winds wrong.

Maybe they were stronger than anticipated. Straining his eyes, he continued peering out through the windshield. Finally, after what seemed like half an hour, the Middle Keys came into view. "Over there!" the copilot shouted, pointing about fifteen degrees to starboard. In the distance, the tiny islands could be seen as dark voids against the water's shimmering moon-glow. Pointing again, this time a few degrees to port, he added, "The Seven Mile Bridge is over there. That's our mark. Marathon's the long island off to the right of it. Damn...right on the money!"

The captain acknowledged the sighting with an almost undetectable nod of his head. He checked his watch. It was 4:37 in the morning. Reaching down into his flight bag, he felt for his gun, reassuring himself that it was still there, ready to be used at a moment's notice. Then, not wanting his uneasiness to show through, he slowly withdrew his hand from the flight case, leaving the .357 braced between his Jep charts and a thermos. Nervously, he scratched at his chest.

"Three-one-five degrees oughta get us over the bridge," instructed the copilot as he mentally plotted a new course for the Lodestar.

"Three-one-five it is." Gently, the captain initiated a turn towards the bridge.

The copilot was checking a Miami sectional chart with a red-lensed flashlight. "There's powerlines along there. Along the bridge, I mean. I'm not sure how high, though." The high-tension lines were not indicated on the chart. The experienced aviator was speaking strictly from memory.

The captain heeded the warning by influencing the heavily loaded airfreighter up another hundred feet. Might as well play it safe. No point taking any chances at this stage of the game, he mused in the back of his brain.

Things were deadly enough as they were with the tons of marijuana in the cabin.

Still scrutinizing the chart, the copilot's eyes were drawn to an area of restricted airspace located about eighteen nautical miles to the west of the Seven Mile Bridge, directly over Cudjoe Key. The airspace was home to *FAT ALBERT*, an unmarked tethered balloon carrying "Look-Down" Doppler radar. Although the balloon was used for spotting low-flying aircraft trying to sneak into the country below the coverage of normal ground-based radar, the right-seat pilot was not worried. Falcon had taken care of everything. Falcon always took care of everything. It was imperative. The organization's survival depended on it. Falcon, after all, controlled one of the largest marijuana importation rings in the United States.

It had been easy for Falcon to get his pilots the window through the government's radar net. All it took was money. Lots of money. Cash money. Everybody had their price. For some, it was $5,000. Others held out for larger amounts—$15,000, $25,000, even $50,000 depending on the value of the information.

That had been the price of tonight's intelligence. Fifty thousand green ones. In exchange for the cash, Falcon had received a message. Short and simple, it had read *FAT ALBERT INOPERATIVE TONIGHT*. But those four words meant a great deal to Falcon and to the two pilots flying the Lodestar over the Florida Keys. It meant safety. It meant free skies. It meant profits.

The message told them that the Aerostat radar balloon at Cudjoe Key was down for maintenance. Images of low-flying aircraft were not being sent to radar screens in Miami—not tonight. The Lockheed Lodestar was free to go about its clandestine business as planned, flying straight towards the bridge, just south of

Marathon.

The Overseas Highway became clearly visible as the aircraft drew closer to it. Then, as the Lodestar passed over the bridge, the captain put the plane through a series of Dutch rolls. Together, both flyers kissed the Atlantic good-bye and welcomed in a new body of water—the Gulf of Mexico.

"If this ain't like fucking the government right up its ass, then I don't know what is!" exclaimed the copilot, which he followed with a hearty laugh. He then turned around in his seat to face a third man sharing the cramped cockpit with himself and the captain.

The man was of a darker complexion than the pilots—not negro, but Latin. A solid gold bracelet was clasped around his right wrist, inscribed with the name *GUSTAVO* in large bold letters. A diamond-studded gold Rolex adorned his left wrist. He was Falcon's trusted courier—the man responsible for seeing that the load arrived safely in Florida.

If Gustavo had spoken five words of his broken English during the entire all-night flight up from Colombia, it would have been a lot. But the twenty-four year old Colombian national remained quiet in his seat as the Lodestar droned on towards its destination.

Buckled snugly to the worn leather cushion of the cockpit jumpseat, directly behind the flight crew, Gustavo was feeling edgy. He sensed something, although he didn't know what. Not wanting anything to go wrong, he rested his nimble fingers on a MAC-10 automatic pistol, which was tucked awkwardly in the waistband of his pants. The powerful weapon was much too big to be carried the way he had it, but that's where he kept it. Pure Latin machismo.

The copilot said to Gustavo, "That intelligence crap sure pays off nicely, don't it?"

For no apparent reason, except maybe for his extreme edginess, Gustavo came alive from the flyer's remark. He drew the MAC-10 from his pants and pressed the weapon against the copilot's skull. "My friend, you flys only. You no talks to me." Then, just as fast as the automatic pistol was drawn, it was quickly and efficiently pushed back into Gustavo's waistband. A grin was plastered on his face. "I scares you?" he asked.

There was no answer from the copilot. He was too terrified to even open his mouth, let alone speak.

"I scares you." This time it was a statement of fact. "You turns around and flys dis plane."

The copilot did just that, turning away from Gustavo and setting his eyes once again upon the aeronautical chart laid out on his lap. From there, he gazed up at the instrument panel where he scanned a breadth of dials and gauges, half of them no longer working from old age. Then his eyes quickly glanced back down at the chart, then out the windshield and finally, he settled his sight on the lighted panel. He was now as nervous as the captain. He thought about the rip-off. Damn, he wished the captain would give him the signal already. He wanted to get it over and done with.

Fifteen minutes slipped by before the captain reached forward and turned a worn black knob on the panel, dimming the instrument lights. Although this made it somewhat difficult to read the gauges, it was a necessary part of the plan.

It was also the signal the copilot had been waiting for. It was time. The copilot looked over towards the captain. "Final heading is three-four-five. That oughta bring us straight over Charlotte Harbor. We'll follow the ADF in from there."

The Lodestar's captain banked the aircraft into a shallow turn to the north, then leveled off the plane on the correct heading of 345^0. The scheduled destination, as arranged by Gustavo, was a rarely used dirt road near the coastal town of Punta Gorda. The brazen pilots, however, were not counting on landing there. They had another site in mind.

Over the next few minutes, the captain allowed the Lodestar to deliberately drift off course...past 347^0 on the magnetic compass...past 350^0...past 355^0. He finally fixed the course on 358^0. Straight ahead lay rural LaBelle, a quiet farming community southwest of Lake Okeechobee. It was there that the pilots were planning to set the plane down on a freshly plowed cucumber field, some twenty-five miles to the east of Punta Gorda.

For their plan to work, it was a must that Gustavo not get a good look at the dimly-lit instrument panel. It was imperative that Gustavo not suspect a thing. Both pilots knew they had to act as natural as possible for the rip-off to go down successfully. And if it did, Falcon's profits would be theirs to split. Instead of two million dollars for Falcon and $100,000 for each of them, it would be two million for them. It was a risky venture, but worth every bit of the gamble.

For the next half-hour, the cockpit remained relatively quiet—almost peaceful. The .357 Magnum was continually on the captain's mind. He kept anticipating its usage. He still wasn't sure if he could kill a man in cold blood. Finally, he knew the time had come. With his left hand remaining firmly on the control wheel, he reached into his flight bag for...

...the flash was blinding, the echo deafening as Gustavo fired off several rounds from his MAC-10 into the captain's heart from behind. Blood and body tissue splattered against every inch of the stale cockpit.

The copilot, although sickened by the horrendous sight surrounding him, instinctively grabbed for the wheel and took control of the aircraft. In less than three seconds, the Lockheed Lodestar had descended almost into the sea. Gradually, the flyer regained most of the plane's lost altitude. But things were not looking good for him. He could feel the still-hot gun barrel of the MAC-10 being pressed smartly against the back of his neck.

With authority, Gustavo told the copilot, "Now you lands where I says. Now you flys to Punta Gorda."

The frightened aviator had no choice but to follow Gustavo's demand. He banked and turned the plane to the left, setting the airfreighter on a course for Punta Gorda.

A short while later, over Charlotte Harbor, a radio signal was picked up on the Automatic Direction Finder from the landing site's portable ADF station. The copilot tracked inbound on the invisible electronic beam until he spotted car headlights marking the dirt road in the distance. With two miles to go, he eased back on the power levers, lowered the flaps and then the gear. All lights were indicating green. Touchdown was moments away.

Sweating profusely, the copilot fought as best he could to maneuver the slow-flying airfreighter through the dark nighttime sky, but the controls felt sluggish in his hands, preventing any bit of real precision. Considering the circumstances, though, he was doing a hell of a job handling the plane.

Seconds later, the Lodestar hit the ground with a loud thud of rubber on dirt. The engines were shut down as the plane came to a full stop in the middle of the road. Several four-wheel drive vehicles were standing by with ground crew, all of them eager to begin off-loading the bales of pot from the late arrival.

Meanwhile, up in the cockpit, Gustavo shot and killed the copilot by piercing the flyer's brain with a round of bullets from his MAC-10. Then, to satisfy his ego, Gustavo fired off two more shots—this time with his Nikon 35mm. Once developed, the pictures would be added to the Colombian's grotesque photo collection of lives he'd eliminated in the line of duty.

Before exiting the cockpit, Gustavo had one final chore to complete. Reaching forward, he yanked the black falcon charms from around the necks of both dead flyers, removing the only evidence linking the crime to the organization.

With his job done for the day, Gustavo left the aircraft and walked towards a vehicle waiting to rush him back to Miami, all the while contemplating his next assignment—finding replacements for Falcon's two dead crewmen. He knew the task would not be a difficult one, for there were so many fools in this world. So many fools.

CHAPTER ONE

November - Friday Morning

Robert Jensen stared out at the aging Douglas DC-4 from the rear seat of the black and white taxi as the cab pulled onto the ramp at Houston Intercontinental Airport. The tramp airfreighter looked uninviting. Almost as uninviting as life itself.

For someone who had only been around for twenty-nine years, Rob Jensen had seen a lot—much of it not good. His mind and body were tired, his emotions distraught. Many times he had wanted to pack everything in and say, "To hell with it all." End his life. Suicide.

But he never did. Something always came up that needed doing. A left-seat flying job. A favor for Maureen. Something. And so, just barely, Rob kept on with his life—breathing, flying, maintaining his six-foot-two-inch body the best he could.

It was possible, of course, that deep down Rob really didn't want to die. Perhaps his thoughts were just bent towards the extreme. Not that it mattered much. The fact was, the suicidal tendency was there. Rob knew it. The deadly act was always roaming the far reaches of his mind, occasionally creeping forward.

Through the cab's dirt-tinted windows, Rob glanced

up at the deep blue sky. Above, there was nothing but a few wispy, feather-like cirrus clouds suspended high in the southeastern quadrant.

Rob rolled down the side window and breathed heavily. The air was crisp and light with no hint of smog. It was a perfect day for flying. Perfect in all respects but one—Rob didn't feel like flying.

Despite his personal feelings, however, he knew he had to fly. It was his job to ferry the beefy airfreighter down to Opa Locka Airport in South Florida. The black falcon charm around his neck reminded him of it. The man named Falcon demanded it. And Gustavo would most definitely be at the airport to make sure of it.

Rob cursed the day he involved himself with the organization. He cursed Falcon. He cursed Gustavo. He cursed the whole damned world—except for Maureen. Why had Gustavo's "come-on" of making a hundred grand for one night's work been so tempting?

It was the fucking bass, Rob thought. That was the answer. Bass and the goddamned cargo operators he'd been flying for, bringing home less than $15,000 a year after taxes. That's why he'd done it. That's why he'd fallen for Gustavo's lines. He was going to make the one dope run, take his cash and leave the pressures of society behind. He was going to sell his mobile home—buy a cabin out in the sticks somewhere. He was going to spend more time bass fishing. Fuck that noise, though. Falcon had forced Gustavo to shove more runs down his throat, with the constant threat of death being the retainer.

And so, here he was in Houston, Texas, almost nine months to the day. He still didn't own the cabin in the woods. The tin-can trailer was still in his name, mortgaged to the hilt. At least he'd kept his promise of doing more fishing. And he had a spanking new, top-of-the-line bass boat sitting in his driveway, paid for with cash—dirty money. Rob cursed Falcon again as the taxicab pulled closer to the plane that needed ferrying.

Riding in the back of the cab with Rob, sitting motionless, was Nick Donovan, Rob's copilot for the flight to Florida. Twice Rob's age and three times as scruffy, Nick also didn't give a damn about piloting the DC-4 parked out there on Houston's ramp. His reason, though, wasn't the same as Rob's, for Nick put up with flying for Falcon. The work was exciting and the high pay supported his many habits. Nick's reason was simply that his mind was someplace else, lost in a fantasy world as he watched a Boeing 747 gracefully liftoff from the runway, probably headed for some faraway destination. It should have been him strapped in the spacious cockpit of that jetliner, his jacket sleeves proudly displaying four gold captain's bars. It should have been him—but it wasn't. Nick had blown his chance long ago when he had let alcohol and a non-conformist attitude put a damper on his career with a major South American airline.

Now, here he was pushing sixty years of age with a graying beard and wrinkles, still copiloting the same junk he flew back in the 1940's and 50's. The same types of airplanes that had cost him his left foot in the crash down in Brazil—old, radial-engined transports. The DC-4's ...DC-6's...Lodestars...Beech-18's. They were all basically the same. Flying death traps. That's what they were. Flying death traps. But they were all Nick had, so he stuck with them.

When the taxi finally pulled up next to the airplane, Rob handed the driver a twenty dollar bill for the $4.50 fare. "Keep the change," he said generously as he and Nick exited the cab.

The driver stuffed the bill into his shirt pocket, lit a cigarette and sped away, leaving the two pilots alone with their airplane.

But Rob and Nick were not alone. From across the ramp, a short man with jet-black hair approached them. As he neared, it was apparent he had a gun stuffed into the waistband of his pants. The man was no stranger to the two pilots.

"*Buenos dias,* my friends!" It was Gustavo in all his splendor. A racing jacket matching the color of his dark, wavy hair was unzipped almost to Gustavo's waist. Diamond-studded cowboy boots and a pair of denim jeans finished off the outfit. Gustavo's usual amount of heavy gold jewelry dangled from his body, including the chain around his neck with the black falcon charm on it. "How flight was?" he asked in his broken English, referring to the commercial flight the two Floridians had taken to get to Houston.

"Fucking male stewardesses," Rob commented defiantly, his crude undertones intended. He never did adjust to the airlines' current trend of presenting male flight attendants to the flying public. After all, what had been so terrible about a nice pair of thirty-eight double-D's walking up the aisle—or at least being served an ice-cold Budweiser by a pretty face with a set of perky A-cups? Rob just couldn't understand the airlines' thinking.

Nick also answered Gustavo's inquiry by grumbling something unintelligible under his breath. Probably something about the change-of-plane layover in Atlanta. Always in Atlanta. Nick hated flying as a passenger on commercial flights. It made him uncomfortable not having control of the aircraft in some way.

Today's flight had been especially torturous for Nick. He'd gotten stuck sitting next to an old lady who insisted on telling him all about her wonderful grandchildren. All eleven of them. And to top if off, the flower-hatted lady had had a wallet that contained a non-ending gallery of family photographs as proof to her borish chatter. Nick hated flying as a passenger.

When the greetings were over between the three men, they got down to business. Nick went off to do the preflight inspection, while Gustavo and Rob discussed the aircraft's overall condition.

"The maintenance logs?" Rob asked quizzically.

Gustavo pointed towards the cockpit, indicating that the books were already inside the airplane. "Is no problems," he insisted. "Plane is good."

"Yeah, that's your opinion. I still wanna see the logs." Rob was eyeing a puddle of grimy oil on the ground beneath the number two engine. It was normal for radial engines to drip oil, but the number two definitely had a major leak. The other three engines looked fine to Rob, with each of the powerplants having only minor puddles to account for.

Rob walked over to the suspicious number two engine, mounted inboard on the left wing. Gustavo followed him over. Together, they examined the evidence.

"I don't know, Gustavo. You may be wrong. I think this plane's got problems. This leak could be serious...or it could lead to something serious." Rob reached up and ran his finger along the bottom of the engine cowling. He thought for a moment as he wiped his oily finger on his shirt. "It could be bad rings...or guides. Maybe we've got a cylinder head that's shot all to hell...who knows? I guess it could be nothing, too. I'll have George open her up tomorrow and take a look." Turning away from the engine and towards Gustavo, Rob asked, "When's our next run to Colombia?"

Gustavo pulled out a folded piece of paper from his left hip pocket. He unfolded it and handed it to Rob. "Here, my friend." It was the logistics sheet for Falcon's next drug flight. "We flys Saturday," Gustavo pointed out.

"No fucking way! That's tomorrow!" Rob exclaimed, shaking his head from side to side.

Gustavo laughed. "I gives you times. We no flys 'til next Saturday."

"Oh...okay, then." Relief was in Rob's voice. "I guess George can do something about the leak by next Saturday. That gives him a week."

"*Si.* George is good mechanics."

"That depends who you ask," Rob responded with sarcasm.

"Ah, my friend. I remembers. You no likes each others."

No comment from Rob. To him, Falcon's mechanic was nothing but a lazy waste of human flesh. Rob, of course, had no say in the decision. For some reason, George was Falcon's choice as the organization's line mechanic. Rob turned his attention back to the logistics sheet, studying the paper attentively.

Gustavo sensed what Rob was looking at and put forth, "You knows where is this Hato Nuevo is? Where we flys to Saturday?" Gustavo's English was getting worse with time. He never was a very good scholastic achiever.

Rob looked up. "I've got an idea of where it's at. I know it's somewhere inland from the coast of the peninsula...somewhere east of Barranquilla...almost near the Colombian-Venezuelan border, I think."

"*Si. Peninsula de la Guajira.* You knows where is this is then. You no loses us."

"I no loses us, Gustavo," Rob kidded. "What about the landing site? Any details on it yet? That last one was pretty marginal."

Gustavo looked over his shoulder to see how Nick was coming along with the preflight inspection, completely ignoring Rob's inquiry about the destination's landing field.

"What about the airstrip?" Rob asked again.

Gustavo turned back to Rob. "I picks good strip. Plenty feets for airplane."

"Yeah, sure." Rob's sarcasm glared through once again. He knew that Gustavo didn't know shit when it came to picking airplanes and that the Latin knew about the same when it came to landing sites. And yet, like George was the mechanic, Gustavo was Falcon's procurement man. Ironic, Rob thought, that as always, the next drug flight was doomed to count heavily on luck. Rob figured he'd probably be able to handle it if the organization was run three-quartered-assed, but half-assed just didn't buy it for him. "Anything else you wanna let me in on?" Rob wanted to know.

"No. I sees you backs at Opa Locka, my friend." Gustavo turned and walked away from the airplane.

When the Latin had gotten about thirty yards distance, Rob called out, "Hey! Is this thing fueled?"

"*Si!*" Gustavo shouted back as he continued walking.

But Gustavo was called at again—this time by Nick. "Man, you suck, Gustavo! This plane is crap!"

Gustavo's reaction was like a bomb going off. He couldn't have gotten any hotter had there been a nuclear detonation on the field. He came storming back to the airplane with hatred in his eyes. Although he was much smaller physically than Nick, he shoved the burly copilot about three feet backwards using his outstretched forearms. He shouted "Look, old mans! I takes you out one days. You keeps talks like this, I kills you."

Nick spoke loudly, too, egging Gustavo on. "Man, without that gun of yours, you'd be nothing but chicken shit."

Gustavo's dark eyes glared forcefully. He barked, "*Maricon!*" He knew Nick understood Spanish. Then, without any regard for the possibility of on-lookers, Gustavo withdrew his gun and threw it wildly to the ground. With nostrils flaring and both hands clenched into muscular fists, he shouted at Nick, "Come. Charge me. I wait for months this fight."

Being an avid barroom brawler, Nick realized his opportunity at getting in the first punch. He lunged forward, landing a few violent blows into the Colombian.

Gustavo staggered away momentarily. He put his hand to his mouth, where he had taken a particularly hard punch from Nick. His lower lip was bleeding. Gustavo soon regained his composure, though. Coming back with vengence, he surprised the flyer with his own style of street fighting, learned a decade ago when he was a member of a teenage youth gang in Cartegena.

Rob kicked the gun—a MAC-10—out of reach of either man, but did nothing to stop the altercation. He stood back and watched the fighting with detached bemusement. He knew the fight was overdue. Each man had been chewing at the other's ego for too long. They were venting anger. Buy why did they have to do it out in the open? What if somebody drove by and spotted the gun? It would raise suspicions—something none of them needed.

The fight lasted another seven minutes before Nick and Gustavo simultaneously called it a draw. Both were out of breath. Both their faces showed battle wounds—open cuts, puffiness, oozing red blood. They stood eye to eye. Their feud was not over. Not just yet.

Gustavo walked away, leaving the two crewmembers to ready Falcon's airfreighter for the flight from Texas to Florida.

The sound of thundering piston engines could be heard reverberating through the morning air as Rob taxied the DC-4 out to Houston's Runway 32. He held the aircraft short of the runway as a Lockheed L-1011 began its takeoff roll down the 12,000 foot slab of concrete.

After a short delay, an air traffic controller said over the radio, "November-Two-Five-Three-Kilo-Yankee cleared for takeoff, runway three-two. Wind three-four-zero at seven. Caution wake turbulence, departing heavy. Immediate right turn to zero-niner-zero VFR approved." Terse and to the point. Each word carried important information to the pilots of N253KY.

"Three-Kilo-Yankee is rolling," Nick said into the mike, acknowledging the radio transmission.

Takeoff power was applied. The aircraft moved forward, constantly building speed. The load was light—no cargo, no passengers.

Minutes later, Rob and Nick were leveled off at 7,500 feet, passing over the Gulf of Mexico after crossing Galveston Bay. A mile long oil slick could be seen on the water's surface in the distance off the airfreighter's left wingtip—modern man's contribution to the environment.

Rob engaged the autopilot, then looked over at Nick. "What made you let loose like that back there in Houston?"

"That machismo little prick called me an asshole and nobody calls me an asshole and gets away with it." As he spoke, Nick picked dried blood from his full growth of facial hair.

"I never heard him call you an asshole."

"Man, that's 'cause you don't speak Spanish. *Maricon*...asshole. Same fucking shit either way."

"Yeah, well, if you keep razing Gustavo like that, you're gonna end up as just another snapshot in his album." Rob waited for a reply. He knew he'd get a good one.

"I hate that Colombian faggot!" Nick fumed, his wrinkles becoming more apparent in his fit of anger.

"Go ahead and hate him all you want," Rob said, in agreement with his copilot's feelings. "But shit, Nick, do it behind his back. Don't flaunt your hatred in the man's face."

"Hey, like I tell the ladies...if you got it, flaunt it. And, man, I got it."

And that was all the two of them said to each other for the next several hours. Then, somewhere over Central Florida, the musty cockpit again became alive with conversation.

Rob was the one who broke the silence. "Shit, I'm starved. A burger, fries and chocolate shake would go good with me right about now." When Nick didn't respond, Rob checked the panel clock. "It's three o'clock already. We won't be on the ground for another two hours. How about if we make an unscheduled pit-stop in Orlando? I'll buy."

"Man, you should've ate that airline food on the way in to Houston. It wasn't that bad. First-class stuff and all."

"You call rubber steak and powdered eggs *not that bad?*"

"Hey, I swallowed mine without puking."

"I swear, Nick. You must have a lead-lined stomach."

"Man, I had to eat. I was so hungry, I was starting to see God."

Pushing Nick's humor aside, Rob asked again, "Well, what about it? Do we go for Orlando?" He was rubbing his stomach to emphasize his suggestion.

"Nah. Let's just get this bird home. You'll live."

"We can tell Gustavo we had a mechanical," Rob offered, still trying to convince Nick of his idea.

"Hey, you're the captain, man. Do what you fucking want. I've already given you my worthless opinion."

Rob knew Nick was right about not landing in Orlando, so he shut his mind off to food. Silence once again filled the cockpit. Although Rob's mood was relaxed, a thick air of invisible tension was building up inside of him as the aircraft continued southward, flying above acres of neatly rowed citrus groves.

A few minutes later, Rob spurted weakly, "I'm getting out."

"What the hell you talking about?"

"From Falcon. From the organization. I'm getting out...after our next run."

"Man, you're fucking crazy. You know you won't do it."

"Fuck you, Nick."

"Yeah, fuck me!" Nick laughed a gutteral laugh that came from deep down inside his diaphragm. He pulled at his beard.

"I'm serious. I'm leaving. I'm escaping. You should, too."

"What for?"

"'Cause we've been in this organization for too long. Falcon's using us. You know it and I know it. We both went into this thing nine months ago to make one run, grab a hundred grand each and get out. But look what's happened. Falcon's already forced four more runs on us. And now this next one. You know when it's gonna end, Nick? It's gonna end when Falcon gets tired of us. He's not gonna want us hanging around here forever, you know. And when the time finally does come that he decides to have Gustavo hire fresh meat, he's gonna have us wasted...just like those bastards before us. That's why we've got to make a break for it now...before Falcon breaks us."

"Man, you're probably right. But I ain't going nowhere."

"Why not?"

"Cause I can't."

"But why?"

"Hey, man! Stop hassling me, okay?"

"Shit, no. You've got to have a reason."

"Life's a bitch and then you die. That good enough reason for you?"

"No."

"Look, man," Nick scorned, turning away from Rob. "I ain't like you." Gazing blankly out the side window, he added, "I ain't young no more. Don't you think I know my own destiny?" Nick then turned back toward Rob. "In a way, I am like you. My life ain't been easy. But then I ain't complaining either."

"Maybe not, but why stick around 'til they slaughter you?"

"Look, this drug shit's risky...sure. But I ain't afraid of it...or of them. I can handle myself. Besides, it's all I got. And the pay is good."

"Christ, Nick. How much fucking more money do you want?"

"How the fuck do I know? What I do know is that I don't wanna talk about it no more, okay? So you go ahead and leave without me. If anybody questions me, I'll make like I don't know nothing."

"Come on, Nick. I've known you a long time. What's really eating at you? Why're you staying?"

"'Cause I ain't got no money stashed away like you do," Nick confessed. "And a sixty year old asshole ain't going no place without no money."

Rob was stunned. "How the hell did you blow three hundred grand in less than a year?"

"Easy," Nick put forth. "Gambling, boozing and

whoring...with about equal shares of each. You know, stuff like flying down to Rio on the Concorde. Shit like that. Believe me, it ain't hard if you try."

"I guess not."

"How much *you* got saved up?" Nick questioned with curiosity as to his buddy's wealth.

"About two hundred of it."

"Two hundred thousand dollars? Two hundred fucking G's?"

"Something like that," Rob answered nonchalantly. "It would've been four if Falcon hadn't stiffed us on the second and fourth runs."

"Fucking A!"

"Yeah, I know."

"So, Mr. Money...what're you gonna do with this two hundred grand? Buy into a business or something?"

"No. I'm gonna use it to escape from the organization...from this nightmare we're in. I've been thinking about it for a long time. It's all planned out."

"Where you escaping to?"

"Don't take this personally, Nick, but I'd rather not tell you. Less chance of Falcon ever finding out that way. Know what I mean?"

Nick nodded in affirmation. "Yeah, man. My mouth talks too much when I drink. And I drink a whole hell of a lot."

"You've got it."

Nick *had* gotten it, but he wasn't finished with his questioning yet. Still probing Rob's up-coming disappearance, he asked, "What about Maureen? You leaving her behind or's she going with you?"

Rob didn't answer. He didn't have an answer. He turned his head sideways and stared out the window at the orange groves seven thousand feet below. Nick had hit upon his Achilles' heel—sweet Maureen. Damn, Rob thought, why did Nick have to bring her into this?

To Rob, Maureen was everything. She was his savior, his stabilizing force, his best friend. She wasn't family, but like family. Like a younger sister. At least that's what he wanted her to think. For all practical purposes, though, Maureen was the only family Rob had. He could talk to her openly and honestly about almost anything. And that was good because Rob was a very closed-off person. His feelings were hidden beneath layers of emotional scars—eight years worth.

As a child, everybody had thought Rob was just an ordinary happy-go-lucky kid with not a care in the world. But oh, how they were wrong. In actuality, Rob had been filled with an unexplainable inner turmoil that never let up. His depression had followed him throughout his teenage years and on into early adulthood. Then, shortly after his twenty-first birthday, a blighted first relationship triggered him into a self-imposed emotional exile. He swore off relationships. He swore off love.

It had taken Rob a long time to build up his emotional barrier—and it had taken Maureen just two years to partially break through it. Rob loved Maureen for that, though he wouldn't admit it to her. He was still afraid of letting his feelings show. Still afraid of getting hurt—of getting burned again.

It was a definite dilemma for Rob—deciding what to do about Maureen. She knew nothing about his escape plan, nor did she even know about his involvement with the drug world. He'd never gotten around to telling her. She still thought he was flying legal cargo runs out of Miami International Airport once or twice a week.

Rob wondered if he even had the right to take Maureen with him—to expose her innocence to his nightmarish existence. He wondered hard, then made a decision. He would explain everything to her—slowly, carefully. Then, he would let *her* choose to either come or stay behind. It was the only way.

She would probably choose to stay, he thought, once she found out he was involved with dope running. Besides, Maureen was due to graduate from college in June with a degree in education, qualifying her to fulfill a life-long dream of landing a real job—teaching—as opposed to the barmaid profession she'd known for so long. Rob didn't think she would give that all up for him. Not once she knew the facts.

In truth, Rob knew he had no right taking Maureen away from her dream. Deep down, though, in his crying heart, he hoped she would choose him.

CHAPTER TWO

Friday Afternoon

The thirty-one foot sailboat sat proudly in the water behind the Baker residence on Royal Palm Drive just north of Las Olas Boulevard in Ft. Lauderdale. The sloop's fiberglass hull, molded in white gelcoat with a light green stripe, reflected nicely off the shimmering waterway. The boat, christened *C'DOCKED'R,* was like a second child to its owner, Dr. Douglas Baker, M.D.

Doug Baker had been involved with sailing all his life—racing dinghies at summer camp, crewing aboard blue-water vessels during college breaks, chartering on weekends during the lean years of building up his medical practice. Ironically—or rather, fortunately—it was his practice that finally allowed him the pleasure and freedom of boat ownership.

Doug had learned long ago about the tranquility of anchoring in an isolated cove, how it cleared the mind of frustration. He had learned, too, the exhilaration of breaking waves in a rough sea and the joy of passing another vessel miles from shore, such as on that rare afternoon when a Brigantine square-rigger passed astern *C'DOCKED'R* with all working canvas hoisted and full.

Such sailing experiences eased the pain in Doug

Baker's life. Pain that came mainly from his sixteen year old daughter's drug addiction. The problems caused by Susan Baker's dependancy carried over onto her father and, at forty-two, Doug was prematurely gray—although, by following a strict regimen of jogging and daily workouts he'd managed to maintain an athletic build.

Doug was aboard *C'DOCKED'R,* fiddling around on deck, preparing the boat for departure which was scheduled for nine in the evening. Climbing onto the coach roof, Doug removed the canvas sail cover, folded it neatly, then moved back to the cockpit, where he stored the cover in one of the seat lockers.

Doug's wife, Maggie, stuck her head out the companionway hatch to catch a breather after having been cooped below all afternoon storing away the bags of groceries and other live-aboard necessities needed for their two-week Bahamian cruise.

Maggie's forty-two years had been better to her than Doug's had to him. Middle-age had not taken away her natural beauty. At least that's what everyone thought. Actually, she owed her ravishing appearance mostly to the miracles of modern science and the skilled hands of her plastic surgeon.

Softly running her slender fingers through her sweat-soaked, brunette-colored hair, she thought contemplatively for a moment, then said to Doug, "I still feel we're making a mistake by taking this cruise. Susan needs to be entered into a fulltime drug rehabilitation program. One run by professionals. This brainstorm of yours is—" Maggie paused briefly, then continued, "It's just so out of line with our normal way of handling problems. We're not facing reality."

"Sure we are, Mag. What you have to keep in mind is that Susan comes from our own flesh and blood. We raised her from infancy. Maybe she's on drugs because of something we did, who knows? In any case, we have to at least try and work this thing out on our own ground first." Doug closed and latched the seat locker. "I know what you're saying about the rehabilitation program, though. If Susan was a patient of mine, that's what I'd recommend to her parents."

"Then why are you resisting it with our own child?"

"I'm not. We've discussed this dozens of times, Mag. If we can't help Susan through withdrawal by the end of this cruise, she's going into rehab. Two weeks...that's all I'm asking for. Two weeks away from school and the pressures of her peers. Two weeks away from the stresses of being a teenager. Susan's agreed to go along with our terms, so what more can we ask of her? It's a start, Mag. A beginning. Something to base a solid foundation on over the next two weeks. Let's at least try."

"I still think we're wrong for taking this cruise."

The Intracoastal Waterway's black inky surface was rippling from the tidal flow on this bustling Ft. Lauderdale Friday night. *C'DOCKED'R's* Westerbeke diesel was idling in neutral as Doug waited patiently for the 17th Street Causeway bridge to open. He passed the minutes studying the classic lines of a fine wooden sailing yacht tied up alongside one of the nearby marinas. He guessed the vessel's overall length was close to one hundred and ten feet, with at least ninety feet on the waterline. The sailboat's ketch rig stood tall above a backdrop of nearly five dozen other sailing and motor yachts docked at the marina.

Doug shifted *C'DOCKED'R's* engine into forward gear, tweaked the throttle and slowly motored towards the wooden vessel. Upon closer inspection, he noticed the sailboat was flying a British ensign from its stern-mounted flagstaff. Doug lost himself in thought, imagining the ecstacy the yacht's crew must have felt during the Atlantic crossing—a blue-water voyage he'd love to attempt someday.

When the causeway's bridge gates came down, stopping the east and west-bound flow of car traffic on 17th Street, Maggie quickly ended Doug's daydream. "The bridge is opening, Douglas."

"Thanks, Mag." With the two hinged spans of roadway opening wide, Doug increased *C'DOCKED'R's* forward speed and steered the sailboat towards the turbulent water beneath the bridge. He seemed almost disappointed that he had to leave the sight of the wooden vessel behind in *C'DOCKED'R's* wake. Doug had fallen in love with wooden boats when he was twenty-three years old and had crewed for a summer aboard a seventy-six foot gaff-rigged schooner. Ever since, he had promised himself that when he retired, he would buy a wooden boat of classic design and sail around the world like Joshua Slocum. In his mind and in his heart, the dream was still very much alive.

Passing underneath the two raised bridge spans, Doug sucked in the cool night air and thought it refreshing. He looked over at his wife who was sitting nervously across from him in the boat's cockpit. "The forecast is looking good, Mag," he reassured her.

Maggie was sweating terribly. Although she was an experienced sailor, a slight fear always overcame her just prior to setting sail on a long cruise, especially a night crossing to the Bahamas. She knew how unpredictable the Gulf Stream could be at times.

Doug continued with the forecast. "We're certainly not going to break any speed records tonight. The winds are southeast at nine knots. Pretty light stuff. We'll head due east on starboard tack, letting the current set us north toward Great Isaac Light. Then, when we have the lighthouse in sight, we'll turn south, just east of the Stream and make our way to Bimini along the bank on port tack."

"What about rain?" Maggie asked nervously.

"We should see clear skies throughout the night, but there's a twenty percent chance of some early morning showers. Nothing to worry about, though."

"Good." Maggie stood up in the cockpit, clutching the aluminum boom to brace herself. Her apprehension was easing somewhat with Doug's reassurance. "Anyone care for something warm? I've got a steaming thermos of hot chocolate down below in the galley."

A cup of chocolately warmth sounded delicious to Doug. "Yes, please."

"Me too, mom," Susan shouted back from the bow, where she was sitting with her legs dangling loosely over the sides, her hands holding onto the pulpit.

"Okay, that makes the three of us. Be right back." Maggie disappeared down the companionway.

As Doug motored *C'DOCKED'R* through the Port Everglades basin, he gazed forward towards the bow, watching as Susan playfully teased her bare feet in the sailboat's bow wake. It didn't seem possible that the beautiful teenage girl focused in his eyes before him—his daughter—could be a drug addict. She seemed so innocent, so at peace, carefree and child-like. Doug wished he could stop time and keep the moment forever.

He wondered secretly whether his parenting of Susan had anything to do with her addiction. Maybe if he had spent more time with her she wouldn't have found the need to turn to drugs. He didn't know the answers, but hoped he'd find out by the end of the cruise.

Maggie came back up on deck with two cups of hot

chocolate. One for herself, the other for Doug. She'd already handed one out to Susan through the forward hatch.

The next fifteen minutes flashed by with *C'DOCKED'R* motoring out the cut and leaving behind the reflections of Ft. Lauderdale's brightly lit skyline. Once past the rolling motion of the dredged channel, the waves settled down to a gentle one to three feet as forecasted. It was at that point, just beyond the whistle buoy, that Doug and Susan hoisted the mainsail and light-air one-fifty genoa, while Maggie manned the helm. Then, after trimming both sails close-hauled on starboard tack, Doug shut down the Westerbeke diesel, bringing on the transition from power to sail.

An eerie quietness took over as the sails, reacting with the wind, worked their magic to move *C'DOCKED'R* through the water. Except for the sound of water rustling against the hull, Doug listened to the silence as the sloop made two and a half knots of headway towards the Bahamas. This was the peaceful way, he surely thought as his mind flushed away all its tension. Slow, but steady. This was the natural way.

The endless hours of the Gulf Stream crossing passed quickly. The night slipped away. Maggie and Susan had gone below to get some sleep shortly after *C'DOCKED'R* had set sail off the Ft. Lauderdale coastline. At 2400 hours, Maggie reappeared to stand her four hour watch, with Doug keeping her company until 0100. Susan came up on deck to relieve her mother at four in the morning for the 0400 to 0800 watch. Sunrise was Susan's favorite time of day, with its pastel colors and all.

While her parents slept below in the after cabin, Susan relished the loneness of *C'DOCKED'R's* cockpit as she expertly kept the boat on course. Despite her personal problems, Susan was a good sailor. Her father had taught her plenty about the sport and she was glad that he trusted her at the helm of *C'DOCKED'R*. She knew how much the sloop meant to him.

Dressed only in a pair of loose-fitting slacks and a *Motley Crue* tank-top from the rock band's latest concert tour, Susan was beginning to feel the bite of the cool air. Leaving the helm unattended for half a minute, she raced down into her cabin, retrieved a long-sleeved knit sweater and hurried back up to the cockpit. The sweater warmed her small breasts from the seabreeze.

Susan glanced at her wristwatch. It was four-thirty on the dot. She wondered what time she'd spot Great Isaac Light. She knew from experience that the 152 foot tall lighthouse was visible from a distance of twenty-three miles on a clear night.

With much effort, she tried doing some mathematical calculations in her head, but felt more comfortable with pencil and paper. Again, Susan went below—this time to her father's navigation station.

Coming back on deck with a pad and pencil, she scribbled down various numbers, toying with her knowledge of small boat navigation. *C'DOCKED'R's* log was showing twenty-two miles traveled since departing Ft. Lauderdale—a little less than halfway to Great Isaac. Very slow progress, but at least with the slight increase in wind velocity which had come up fifteen minutes earlier, another unit of speed was now showing on the boat's knotmeter.

Assuming the sailboat maintained its current speed of three and a half knots, Susan quickly estimated her sighting of the lighthouse would be at quarter past five. That gave her forty-five minutes to relax before scanning the horizon for Great Isaac's identifying mark. Having sailed the area many times with her father, Susan knew just what to look for—a flashing white light every fifteen seconds.

Susan engaged the autohelm, leaned back against the cockpit coaming and tilted her head skyward, admiring the brilliant canopy of stars hanging above her. She felt like she was among old friends. The Milky Way was magnificient in all its glory. And Gemini, her astrological sign. Gemini's two bright stars were shining effortlessly above the mast. Next, Susan searched for the Big Dipper, which she found suspended to port with its handle pointing downward. Her favorite constellation was Orion. She especially admired one of Orion's corner stars, Betelgeuse, because of the star's sparkling reddish-pink glow when observed away from the interference of city lights. Gazing up at the twinkling Betelgeuse was like watching a Fourth of July fireworks display.

Finally tiring of the stars, Susan lowered her head and looked out over the ocean. Treasuring the serenity of the surrounding blackness, she pulled a plastic baggie out of her front pocket. In the baggie were a dozen joints and a pack of waterproof matches.

Susan took one of the joints out of the baggie and placed it between her lips. Cupping her hands to block the wind, she struck a match and fired up the joint. She inhaled the marijuana smoke deep into her lungs, where she held it for a long time before exhaling.

Her mouth sensed a dirty, dry taste rather than the sweetness she was used to in marijuana, but "Gainesville Green" had been all she could score at the last minute. It was homegrown weed, most likely, by the taste of it. And its potency wasn't even close to comparing with that of the high-grade marijuana she usually bought—the stuff shipped up from Mexico, Jamaica, Colombia. Even California's crop was better than Florida's weed.

After four minutes of heavy smoking, Susan threw the resin-coated roach into the sea. Slowly, the drug took control of her. As a rush came over Susan's head, the sailboat seemed to lessen its pace through the water. Susan was feeling high—euphoric. Nothing could be better.

For the next half hour, Susan let the autohelm do what it was designed to do while she layed back in the cockpit, contemplating all sorts of things, like having sex with her boyfriend on the fifty yard line of the school's football field.

All too soon, though, the drug's effect wore off. Repositioning herself behind the steering pedestal, Susan disengaged the autohelm and began her search for Great Isaac Light. She spotted it about six degrees to starboard. Anticipation of a colorful sunrise was already building up inside of her—her reward for pulling the early morning watch.

Doug joined Susan in the cockpit at a few minutes before eight o'clock, for he was to guide *C'DOCKED'R* the rest of the way in to Bimini. Having balanced two cups of coffee up the companionway, he handed Susan the sugared stuff, keeping the black mud for himself. He'd seen no reason pouring Maggie a cup. She was still sound asleep in the after cabin, despite the sun's morning light flooding in through the cabin's two portholes.

Doug watched for a moment as a seagull circled overhead making screeching shrills, begging for a free handout. Then, looking out over the bow along the horizon and seeing no land in sight, he picked up binoculars and searched diligently for any hint of Great Isaac Light in the sun's blinding glare. He knew it was out there. He just couldn't see it. "How long ago did you sight Great Issac?" he asked Susan.

"It was at five-twenty-five, daddy. We'll need to tack soon...to the south."

"I thought we'd be a little closer by now."

"We're not that far away. We can probably make Bimini in about three to four hours."

"Fine."

On a good day with no haze, the tall Casuarina Pine trees lining Bimini became visible from seven miles out. At that distance, however, the trees looked like thin, dark bands floating above the horizon, their shapes not yet discernible. It wasn't until the boat got nearer to the subtropical island that Bimini became clearly focused to the naked eye.

"It's been really peaceful out here, daddy. You should've come up sooner. A couple of porpoises were playing in our bow wake awhile ago." Steering the sailboat with her feet propped up on the wheel, Susan sipped her coffee, clutching the warm cup with both hands.

Doug looked into his daughter's eyes, then up at the starboard spreader where a yellow flag was waving in the breeze. "I see you've already raised the quarantine flag."

"I know the rules, daddy. I've sailed here before."

"I know. I'm just surprised you're on top of things this morning, that's all."

"Why? You're the one who taught me everything. You're the one who always told me to be a thinking sailor...to be ahead of the game."

"That's not what I'm referring to, Susan."

"Then...what?"

Doug wore a concerned expression on his face. He knew his suspicion about Susan was correct, but he didn't want to approach her out-right with it. Instead, he wanted her to admit to her wrong doing. Collecting his thoughts, he asked, "Don't you have something for me?"

Susan simply replied, "I don't understand," and turned her head away.

"Alright, then. Let me try this from a different angle." Doug made a hand gesture as if he wanted to emphasize a point, but changed his mind before opening his mouth. A third tactic came into his head and he decided it was the better approach. "Susan, what have I always told you about boat people that made them different from everyone else?"

Instead of responding to the question, Susan busied herself by gazing over the port rail, ignoring her father's serious intentions. When the porpoises reappeared beside the boat, she screamed with excitement, "Look! They're back! See, I told you they were here!"

In loving anger, Doug yelled, "I'm trying to get through to you for your own good, Susan! Now pay attention to me!"

"How can I when you're not making any sense?"

"Young lady, let me worry about making sense. You just pay attention and answer my question."

"What question?"

"About boat people...what makes them different?"

"They like boats," Susan answered belligerently.

"I'm not looking for sarcasm, Susan."

"Then I don't know."

"I'm really disappointed in you. Your mother was right about this cruise."

"What do you mean by that, daddy?"

"We're not even twelve hours into the sail and already I'm at a loss for words as to how to handle your drug problem. I've finally realized I'm not qualified in the field of drug rehabilitation. Your mother was absolutely right. Our only alternative is to place you in a drug treatment center."

"But, daddy!" Susan knew she'd been caught.

Reaching into her pocket, she pulled out the baggie and handed it over to her father.

"Is this everything?"

Susan shook her head indicating that it was as she watched her father dump the baggie's contents overboard. "How'd you know, daddy? Was it my eyes?"

"No, it wasn't your eyes...although, they are quite bloodshot."

"Then how *did* you know?"

"Susan, right now in my life, I'm a medical doctor by profession. But in my heart and soul, I'm a boat person first and foremost. I've always dreamed of one day going to sea...of circumnavigating the globe on a sailboat. Someday I'm actually going to do it. In the meantime, I've spent years training myself for the harsh conditions the sea can offer...both mentally and physically. You see, Susan, it's a must for a sailor to be able to perceive his total environment much more so than it is for the average person, especially while sleeping. The sea doesn't forgive anything less than complete awareness and respect. Because of this, I've become adept at noticing even the sublest changes of weather, sea conditions, noises, vibrations...smells."

"Oh...that's why you asked me about boat people."

"Yes." Doug took control of the helm as Susan scooted out of the way. "I'm really disappointed in you," he told his daughter once again.

"Are you gonna tell mom?"

"I'm not sure yet. She'd want me to turn *C'DOCKED'R* around and head for home...which probably isn't such a bad idea considering you broke your promise to us. On the other hand, I don't see any point wasting this cruise. We're already here and it'll give us all a chance to talk as a family. That's something we haven't done in a long time." Doug sipped from his mug, then remarked, "I'll make my decision when we reach Bimini."

CHAPTER THREE

Saturday morning

The telephone woke Rob up as he lay naked on his waterbed, sprawled out without even a sheet for cover. Why the hell were people always waking him up so early in the morning? Why were they always calling him? The Jaycees...the Police Benevolent Association...damn phone solicitors. There should be a law against it. Fucking phones.

With Rob's phone already on its seventh ring and its mad, piercing tone driving him nuts, he reached toward the nightstand for it, but it wasn't there. Rolling over to the edge of the bed, he looked around and saw that the phone had somehow ended up on the floor during the night. He slipped out of bed and grabbed the receiver. "Yeah?"

"Where you at, man? You still sleeping?" Nick had a way with dumb questions.

"What the fuck you calling here so early for?" Rob fumed in anger. His digital clock was showing 11:47 with the alarm not set to go off until one in the afternoon. Rob was not an early riser—not if the bass weren't biting.

"Hey, man. You were suppose to be out here with me and George by eleven...remember...airport...oil leak...test-flight? You with it today or what?"

"Shit!" Rob had forgotten all about the test-flight. He'd had more pressing matters on his mind—his escape plan and Maureen. "I'll be there in forty-five," he told Nick without much enthusiasm. Then, after slamming the receiver back down onto its cradle, Rob crawled back into bed for another fifteen minutes.

A fresh, easterly breeze was blowing across Opa Locka Airport, causing the stench from an on-site sewage treatment plant to be carried across the open expanse of land. It was a scorcher of a Saturday afternoon.

Sharing the acreage at the airfield were half a dozen flight schools, aerial charter outfits, the Coast Guard Air Station Miami and a multitude of aircraft refueling and maintenance operations. Also at the airport was the DC-4 from Houston, which was parked inconspicuously among a gathering of other relic airfreighters on the airport's northeast ramp.

A flaming and splendorous sun was reflecting intensely off the DC-4's weather-beaten sides. With its last paint job having been completed back in 1966, the airfreighter appeared almost sickly. But despite its outward appearance and age—having been built at the Douglas Aircraft factory during World War Two—N253KY was still airworthy.

Like yesterday, Rob was sitting in the cockpit of the plane, mastering the airfreighter's controls from the left-seat. He had all four of the Pratt and Whitney Twin Wasp radials idling nicely at 1,000 RPM. With the parking brakes set, the DC-4 stood motionless on the grease-stained ramp.

Rob looked natural and comfortable sitting behind the controls of a transport-sized aircraft. Tall and lean, he resembled the typical Hollywood motion picture aviator. He wasn't a bad looking guy. His physique was solid muscle and bone. His posture was strong. His hair was dirty-blond. Rob had presence.

His clothes, however, distracted from his otherwise powerful image. Unlike his copilot, who enjoyed dressing up in the airline industry's standard uniform of black pants, black leather shoes and white shirt with shoulder epilets, Rob preferred casual dress. Shorts and a T-shirt suited him fine—or jeans and an old sweatshirt if that's what the weather called for.

Clothes didn't matter much to Rob. His closet and dresser drawers were testimonial to that, for they were stuffed full with a dozen pairs of jeans and at least six dozen T-shirts, each emblazoned with a silk-screened printing advertising everything from a bait and tackle shop to a local tavern, from an aircraft service center to an outboard motor repair facility. That's what he felt comfortable wearing, so that's what he wore. T-shirts. Simple. Basic.

"Man, that sun's a mother today," Nick swore honestly from his usual right-seat position, beads of perspiration dripping from his tan-hide forehead. As each of the moisture droplets cascaded down Nick's leathery face, they became entrapped in his beard, causing the bushy mass to sparkle in the afternoon's golden rays of sunshine.

Nick was a large man. Not tall, but broad shouldered and heavy-set. He carried around at least thirty-five extra pounds of weight in his rotund beer-belly—a beer-belly he was proud of, for he enjoyed bragging how he could out-drink anybody. And he could. He had won countless challenges over that bet in bars the world over. To date, he had racked up not a single loss.

Nick was staunch as well. To him, flying was a man's

game. No place for pussymeat—be it male or female. Flying was a challenge against death. A challenge he'd already beaten once—down in Brazil when he lost his foot. In all the years since that crash, he'd never once allowed his artificial limb to stop him from flying—although, it had kept him out of the captain's seat.

"Let's get this bitch in the air already," Nick demanded of Rob. "It'll cool us down." There was much irritation laced in Nick's voice and plenty of reason for it. With the plane being unairconditioned, he had removed the four over-wing emergency panels to allow fresh air to circulate within the DC-4's cabin. But as long as the plane remained on the ground, the openings were worthless, for the heat was just too overwhelming.

"Okay, then. Let's go," Rob agreed, brushing his hand through the curls of his dirty-blond hair. "I still think this test-flight's a waste of time, though." He turned around to face Falcon's mechanic, who was sitting behind him in the jumpseat. "If you'd just gone and pulled the plugs this morning like I'd asked you to last night, you'd probably already have an answer to the oil leak. You're not gonna find a damned thing wrong with the engine in the air. The instrumentation for number two checked out normal all the way down from Houston."

George took offense to Rob's comments. Poking Rob in the back, he asked sarcastically, "Who's the mechanic around here, bud? You or me?" George and Rob had held a mutual dislike for each other since their first meeting.

"I'm serious, George. This flight's not gonna prove anything. If you'd just—"

"Eat shit and die," growled the mechanic, cutting Rob short.

"You know something...you're the sorriest excuse for a wrench turner I've ever met," Rob shrugged before turning back around to face the instrument panel.

George ignored Rob's remark. He knew he wasn't a lousy mechanic. True, he was lazy—a condition that had plagued him throughout his career. But he wasn't a "sorry excuse for a wrench turner" as Rob had bluntly suggested. In fact, when motivated, George knew he could be quite good. Good enough to have built his own sportplane from a kit in his spare time, of which he had a lot of. Besides, why would Falcon keep him on the payroll if he wasn't any good at his trade?

Of the three men buckled into the cockpit of N253KY, George had been employed by the organization the longest. In his three years with Falcon, he'd seen pilots come and go—but never leave. They just seemed to disappear. Yet, he was still here. There had to be a reason, George rationalized.

With Rob's go-ahead, Nick adjusted his headset, pushed the mike button and placed a call to ground control, receiving taxi instructions in return. He repeated the instructions to the controller while looking out his side window. Seeing that the right wing was clear, he gave Rob the thumbs-up sign.

Rob checked the clearance on his side of the aircraft, released the parking brakes and applied just enough power to start the DC-4 rolling so that he could test the action of the toe brakes. Rob then taxied the aircraft to the west end of the airfield, where he held N253KY short of the runway. He turned the airfreighter into the wind, centered the nose wheel and reset the parking brakes.

George leaned forward, resting his forearms on the backs of the pilots' seats. He paid close attention to the instrumentation as the two flyers gracefully went through the engine run-up. All indications appeared normal.

When the run-up was complete, Nick took out the *"BEFORE TAKEOFF"* checklist and began reading it out loud, with Rob calling back the responses.

"Boost pump?" Nick shouted over the drone of the engines.

"Set high."

"Trim tabs?"

"Set for takeoff."

The list went on. Following the last item, Nick switched the radio to the tower frequency and gave them a call. "Opa Locka Tower, November-Two-Five-Three-Kilo-Yankee is ready at niner-left."

"Three-Kilo-Yankee, hold for landing traffic."

"Three-Kilo-Yankee, ready and holding," Nick acknowledged.

The holding stretched into minutes as several private aircraft landed in succession. Rob started getting fidgety while waiting for Nick to receive their takeoff clearance. When his mind inadvertently turned to Maureen, he winced in anguish. He didn't want to think about her right now—not when he had to fly. Trying to force Maureen out of his head, he asked aloud, "Nick, did I tell you what happened to me in the 'Glades the other day?"

"You finally catch the big one?" Nick guessed.

"No, not even close. I was out in the 'flats', working the bottom with a purple worm and, after a couple of hours, had a cooler full of black bass. Anyway, I was reeling in this one that fought me like a four pounder. I'd gotten him right up beside the boat, just about to net him. Next thing you know, I was knocked flat on my ass. When I got up to see what'd struck the boat, this twelve foot 'gator was gliding away with part of my bass still hanging out the side of his mouth."

"Survival of the fittest," Nick laughed.

"I'll say," Rob added.

The radio crackled in Nick's headset. "Three-Kilo-Yankee, cleared for takeoff, runway niner-left," came the controller's husky voice.

Nick acknowledged the transmission, then told Rob, "Go for it."

Rob added power to the engines and taxied the aircraft onto the runway. Thoughts of Maureen were still bouncing around in his head.

After circling above the Everglades for over an hour, Rob headed N253KY back to Opa Locka Airport. The outcome of the test-flight was as expected. Nothing unusual showed up on the engine instrumentation. Stressing his point to George, Rob put forth, "What'd I tell you? Are you convinced now that you have to start pulling the plugs?"

"Hell, no," George rebutted. "Why should I go tearing apart the engine when there's nothing wrong with it?"

"What are you talking about *nothing wrong*? That puddle of oil we left at Opa Locka is less than twenty-four hours old. And there's another puddle on the ramp in Houston."

"That's your reason?" George argued.

"No. Because I'm the captain of this airplane—that's my reason!"

"Well, excuse me, bud! Didn't know you were so touchy today."

The DC-4 continued on towards the airport. After an uneventful landing, Rob taxied the aircraft back to the northeast ramp, where he shut down the engines and set the parking brakes.

George was the first one out the aircraft. He walked over to a grassy area near the edge of the ramp and picked up four wooden 4x4's. He carried them back to the airplane and used the blocks of wood to chock the main tires.

Rob, after exiting the airfreighter and climbing down the aluminum ladder, walked over to George. "You think you'll get the engine ready by next Saturday?"

"Look, bud! Don't you go worrying about me, okay? If Falcon didn't think I was doing a decent job of it, I'd be out on the street like *that!*" George said, cracking his knuckles for emphasis. But since I'm still here, I figure I do alright by Falcon's standards. So if you don't like the way I go about my business, that's just tough shit!"

"I wasn't insinuating anything, George. But you're acting like there's nothing wrong with that engine. It's not your life that depends on it. Nick and I are the ones who have to fly the plane down to Colombia and back. And we've already put a plane down short of our intended airfield because of one of your oversights. It's not something we'd like to repeat again."

"When? Which plane? I don't remember anything going down because of a mechanical."

"That DC-3 you worked on a couple of months back. The one with the Papa-Tango registration. Luckily for us, we were flying over Belle Glade and were able to set it down in the middle of a sugar cane field. Gustavo managed to get a ground crew out there before dawn to retrieve the load, so he never made a fuss over the incident. But let me tell you, George, he wasn't exactly praising your ass that night."

"Get off my case." And with that, George walked back to the grassy area, where his silver Eldorado was parked. Before getting into the car, he shot Rob the finger.

"You gonna do something about the engine?" Rob asked from a distance.

"I'll work on it tomorrow, asshole!" After starting the Cadillac's engine, George floored the accelerator, leaving twin trails in the grass and burnt rubber on the tarmac.

As George sped away, Nick drove up in his '65 Mustang convertible, which had also been parked in the grassy area. The car was a show-stopper—a beautifully restored classic painted in metallic green. Although the car's airconditioner was running full blast, Nick had both windows rolled all the way down, as well as the convertible's canvas top. "Get in, Rob. Let's haul butt to the bar and get shit-faced. I'll drop you back here later to pick up your Blazer."

"Nah. I'm just gonna head for home. I'll meet you at the bar later on." Rob looked beat. He was tired from a combination of dealing with George, thinking about Maureen and three nights of restless sleep. Most of all, it was the thinking about Maureen. He still could not shake her from his mind. Something had to be done. And fast. Real fast.

CHAPTER FOUR

Saturday night

The *Flight Deck Lounge*, a neighborhood bar owned and run by Philip Jackson, was located about half a mile north of Miami International Airport's eastern perimeter. The bar's decor was anything but classy. In the rear section sat two pool tables, several computer video games and a juke box. The front portion of the tavern consisted of a long, U-shaped counter surrounded by thirty wooden stools, half a dozen well-worn booths set along the east wall and a short-order kitchen near the front entrance. The chef's specialty—if he could be considered a chef—was an onion-steak hoagie and chips for $1.15. When purchased with any domestic beer, the price jumped to a mere $1.75.

The bespectacled Jackson, who preferred being called Jackie, catered mainly to the pilots who worked out of Miami's "Corrosion Corner", an area at the airport set aside for the many tramp airfreighters that still earned their keep flying legal loads of cargo. Roses up from Colombia, chickens out to Nassau, fresh seafood up from the Caribbean, relief flights to and from hurricane disaster areas. Anything, anywhere, anytime—that was the life of a "Corrosion Corner" cargo pilot. Jackie understood their ways, their attitudes, their restlessness. He had once been one of them.

These "nonsked" pilots were a rugged bunch of guys—mostly older men no longer able to pass the rigorous flight physicals demanded by the major airlines. But a trend was being set in "Corrosion Corner". Many younger pilots were taking to the skies in the old transports. Sometimes it served as a breeding ground for bigger and better flying jobs, like the majors. Other times not, leading the young men down deadends.

Although pilots made up the majority of Jackie's customers, they were not the only patrons of the bar. Other regulars included a mixed group of mechanics, a scattering of lower-level airline management types and even an occasional stewardess. The *Flight Deck* also seemed to draw a few middle-aged divorcees seeking sexual adventures. And Jackie, being the warm-hearted person that he was, played father-figure equally to them all.

Nick was standing near the center of the bar with an empty Heineken bottle in his right hand and a lit Marlboro jammed between his lips. He was admiring the firm derriere of Maureen, one of Jackie's nighttime barmaids, who was serving drinks farther on down the counter. As Nick eyed the blond-haired beauty, his mind flowed with carnal thoughts. Rob was a fool, he thought. This babe had the hots for him. All the regulars at the bar knew Maureen would fuck Rob in a minute if he'd give her the chance. But for some ungodly reason, Rob wouldn't let Maureen touch him—at least not in the way a normal, hormone-filled man would. Sure, they'd kissed on occasion. Sissy stuff, Nick mused. He thought that if he ever got the opportunity, he'd nail Maureen good.

"Maureen, baby!" Nick boisterously shouted across the counter. "I need another greeny!"

After taking care of her other customers, Maureen came over. "What was that, Nick?"

"Another Heiney will do fine, darlin'. And a smooch." He puckered his mouth, causing the Marlboro to dangle precariously from his lips. Nick was drunk.

"Sorry, Nicky. Just sold the last one."

"Last one? We talkin' kiss or Heiney here?"

"Kiss."

"Yeah, until Rob gets here. Then you'll be all over him like a little puppy dog."

She ignored the rude statement, turning away instead to get Nick his beer. When she returned with the chilled bottle of Heineken, she caught a glimpse of Rob walking in through the tavern's side entrance. She waved to Rob, but apparently he didn't see her.

Maureen watched as he strolled over towards the juke box, deposited two quarters and punched up several songs. She guessed they were probably Southern Rock and Roll tunes. Rob liked that kind of music—*The Marshall Tucker Band, Lynyrd Skynyrd, Molly Hatchet, The Allman Brothers.* Jackie always kept a few of their songs in the juke as a special favor to Rob.

Maureen kept her eyes upon him as he walked up to the bar counter. "Hey, cutie," she said cheerfully, greeting him as he sat down on the stool next to where Nick was standing.

"Hi." Rob leaned across the counter and gave her a soft kiss on the cheek. He looked into Maureen's eyes, then at her smile. "How're things going tonight? Looks pretty slow for a Saturday."

"It is. Jackie says some of the guys from EuroAir are working overtime to fix a maintenance problem on one of their Treestars. I think that's what he called it."

"Tri-Star," Rob corrected. "A Lockheed L-1011."

"Yeah, that was it! You're so smart, Rob. You know

every plane."

Rob shrugged his shoulders. He had never felt comfortable accepting compliments.

Maureen went on, "I don't know why I can't remember any of this aviation stuff working around you guys all the time. Maybe I should read a book about planes, huh?"

Nick, who had been eavesdropping, butted in with one of his typical sexist remarks. "Don't you go read nothin' darlin'. We like you just the way you are. Sweet, pretty and scantily clad. You don't need to be gettin' no smarter. It's bad enough that you're already goin' to college, 'cause a woman's place is right here...pourin' drinks and playin' dumb." He threw Maureen a wink as he sucked down half his beer in one swallow. He then let out a loud belch that, in return, received various comments from his friends at the other end of the bar.

Maureen gave Nick a cold stare that could freeze fire. "You're sick!" she said in disgust. She then turned back to Rob. "Are you hungry? The kitchen's all closed up, but the cook is still here. I can have him throw together a sandwich for you if you'd like." He didn't so she dropped the idea.

Just then, Rob noticed an open box of long-stemmed roses next to the cash register. He wondered if they were Maureen's. With his curiosity peaked, he looked around for the second barmaid Jackie usually had working on Saturday night. Not spotting her, he asked, "You alone tonight?"

"Except for Jackie and the cook, yeah. Jackie still hasn't hired a replacement for Tamara yet. I can't believe the way she just walked out on us like that last week."

"Oh...yeah. I forgot about that." So the flowers *were* Maureen's, Rob thought. But who would send her expensive roses? Playing innocent, he asked, "Who's flowers?"

"Do you like them?" Maureen's baby-blue eyes were lit up like a child's at Christmas. "I think they're so pretty."

"Then they *are* yours?"

Maureen nodded. "The florist delivered them here about three hours ago. You should've heard everyone in here. This place sounded like a zoo, Rob. They all thought you sent them to me."

Rob swallowed hard, trying to unravel the knot in his throat. He had never sent Maureen flowers. Not that he hadn't wanted to at times. He just couldn't handle it emotionally. Flowers brought up too many bad memories of his last relationship—the one from eight years ago. Shit, he thought, had it really been eight years? It seemed like only last week—or maybe half a year ago at the most.

Rob's thoughts flashed back to the roses. He was about to ask Maureen who they were from when Jackie stepped out of the stock room with a case of liquor and walked behind the counter with it and over to Maureen.

Jackie had a deep, but friendly voice. "Mo, I need you to shelve this booze. Then get started on those glasses." Jackie was tilting his head towards the overflowing sink at the opposite end of the counter.

"Alright. In a second, Jackie." Maureen looked into Rob's eyes and blew him a kiss. "I'll speak to you later, okay? I've been saving my break all night." She blew him another kiss, then walked away to do her chores.

Rob felt like he'd been left out in the cold, still not knowing who sent Maureen the flowers. It ate at him from the inside. His gut wrenched with pain that wasn't there. He wondered if maybe Maureen was seeing somebody beside himself. But if she was, why hadn't she told him?

Nick, who had somehow managed to keep his crude mouth shut for a short while, waited until Maureen was out of earshot range before harshly breaking into Rob's train of thought. "Man, why don't you take her back to your trailer tonight and fuck the shit outta her? You know she wants it. She's got that tickle between her legs. I can tell."

Rob was sickened by Nick's uncalled for remarks. Maureen had done nothing to deserve such verbal abuse, especially behind her back. What Nick needed was to have his front teeth punched out, but instead, Rob just hopped down from the barstool and moved away. He paced to the rear of the bar, then over to the Astro Invaders video game, where he dropped a coin into the machine. For the next couple of minutes, Rob tried venting his anger by blowing up alien spacecraft.

When the animated violence didn't work, he went back up to the bar counter and ordered a beer from Jackie—a Budweiser. Clutching the bottle tightly, as if someone was going to take it from him, Rob moved along to the side of the bar, toward one of the empty booths. He chose the dark one in the corner, underneath the wall-mounted television set. Plopping himself down onto the booth's padded seat, he drank his beer, alone and in silence.

Rob couldn't shake Maureen from his head. What if she *was* seeing somebody else? What then? What would that do to his plans of asking her to come with him on his escape next week? In all his searching, he could find no answers to his myriad questions. All he knew for certain was that Maureen was his only real friend. She was his strength. She was his main reason for wanting to live. She was his one special person in this big, overpowering universe. He didn't know what he'd do if he lost her.

Maureen was indeed a special person. She always

managed to keep a cheerful air about her. Even when her parents had died in a car crash, she had remained up on life. Rob envied her emotional stability.

He also cherished her strong-willed ways. By working six nights a week at the *Flight Deck Lounge,* Maureen had earned enough money to put herself through college. Sometimes when the bills piled up at the end of the month and she struggled to make ends meet in her one-room efficiency apartment, Rob wondered how she could get by without complaining. Yet, she always managed.

Rob tried helping her out financially now and then—much like a brother would. But he could only offer her so much before he'd raise suspicions. After all, Maureen still thought he was flying airfreighters out of "Corrosion Corner" for barely survivable wages.

Damn, he loved her! Why did his past have to continually haunt him? Why couldn't he just put an end to the broken relationship that happened eight years ago? Why couldn't he just get on with his life and tell Maureen that he loved her? Why?

Maureen walked over to her boss and asked for the half-hour break she'd been waiting for all night. When he said, "No," Maureen got stern with him. "I think you're being totally unfair about this, Jackie. I really do. Saturday is my double. I came in even earlier today to set up the grill for you. I worked my entire afternoon shift with only one lousy break and I passed up on dinner so that I could spend some time with Rob. And now you won't even let me do that. I think it stinks."

"Calm down, Mo. Give me a chance to explain. I said you couldn't take a half-hour break. I didn't say you couldn't take a break at all. I thought you understood at six o'clock that if you didn't take it then, you probably wouldn't get as long a break later. We've got those Tri-Star boys coming in soon and they're going to be mighty thirsty."

"That's not my fault!"

"I know it's not. But listen to me, Mo. I need you at the bar." Jackie paused momentarily, trying to think up a compromise between himself and his best barmaid. "I'll make you a deal," he said after awhile. "You go and sit with Rob now...for fifteen minutes. Then later on...after our initial onslaught...I'll give you another fifteen minutes. How's that sound? Fair enough?"

"No, but it's the only choice I've got, isn't it." Maureen was clearly making a statement rather than a question.

"Afraid so, Mo. I'm sorry you misunderstood me before. Rob doesn't usually show up so late. And, Mo...it may not seem like it, but I *do appreciate* the long hours you've been putting in for me lately. It's just that until I find a new girl we're going to be short-handed around here and I've got a business to run."

"Yeah, that's fine. I understand all about the bar business. But what you've got to understand is that it's putting a drain on me. This place isn't my life, Jackie. I've got classes three days a week...and homework...and housework." After a brief lapse, Maureen added, "You've got to hire another girl soon, Jackie. You're not being fair to me." Then, without regard for Jackie, she turned her back on him. As she left the counter area, she snipped, "I'll be back in fifteen minutes. Think you can handle it yourself?" She then paced over to Rob's booth and sat down next to him, still upset.

"What was that all about?" Rob asked, having overheard part of the confrontation.

"Nothing! Just that we can't waste my short break

talking about this slave pit I work at."

"Damn. First Nick and now you. What's everybody getting on my case for?"

Maureen felt truly terrible, for she hadn't meant to push her frustrations off on Rob. She cuddled up close. "I'm sorry, love. I shouldn't have snapped at you like that. It's just that we're never together on weekends anymore and I haven't seen you all week and Jackie...oh, it doesn't matter. I'm here with you now, so let's make the most of it." She reached for Rob's beer and took a sip.

"Drinking on the job?" Rob kidded.

"Ssshhh. Don't tell anyone." Maureen downed a second sip of the icy-cold beer, then put the bottle down and took hold of Rob's hand. "So, love. Where've you been all week?"

"Around...Tampa...Houston."

"Yuck! Sounds boring. No flights down to the tropics?"

"Nah."

Maureen looked deeply into Rob's eyes. "You seem worried," she said, expressing her feelings. "Is something bothering you, Rob?"

"Yeah."

"What's wrong?"

"I guess it's the roses. I've been trying to figure out who they're from."

Maureen's face turned all smiles. "You're jealous, Robert. That's sweet."

"I don't know if I am. I guess it depends on who sent them."

"Well, ease your mind. You've got nothing to worry about."

"Really?"

"Yes, really. You know Jimmy, don't you? The guy who does the airbrushing?"

"Yeah."

"The flowers are from him. He wants me to model for him...for a painting. I haven't given him an answer yet. I've been waiting to get your opinion before making a decision."

"I've seen his work. Some of it gets pretty pornographic...the World War Two type stuff...the nose art."

"But I'd be wearing clothes."

Rob stared at her as if he knew she was stretching the truth.

"Well...sort of," she confessed.

"What kind of 'sort of'?"

"You know, lingerie...bra and panties, garter belt, stockings, high heels. That kind of 'sort of'."

"*No way, Maureen!* What's gotten into you? I can't believe you're even considering doing it."

"I think it'll be fun. Jimmy wants to pose me on the wing of a P-51 Mustang...whatever kind of plane that is. And you *know* how I've always wanted to pose for an artist."

"Jimmy's no artist. Back during the Second World War, he airbrushed nude women on airplanes...that's all. He's just an old, washed-up fighter jock who never outgrew his youth."

"What if I told you the painting is suppose to be a fiftieth birthday present for Jackie from all of us at the bar?"

"Forget it, Maureen! After the way he treated you tonight?"

"But, Rob...Jackie's been good to me over the years. Tonight was just because we were short-handed. I've already calmed down and gotten over that."

"You're crazy."

"Well, if you really don't want me to pose, I won't. But I don't see any harm in it."

Rob scanned the bar with wide-open eyes, then turned his gaze back upon Maureen. "You wouldn't mind working in this dump with all these guys checking out a semi-nude painting of yourself hanging on the wall? Because that's exactly where Jackie would nail the damn thing. Probably on the rear wall by the pool tables."

"I wouldn't mind. I think the regulars would get a kick out of it. Besides, I'll be out of here by August...when I start my teaching job. And as for being semi-nude, mister, I expose more skin at the beach wearing that French bikini you bought me than in what I'd be wearing for the painting."

"Be real! A bikini isn't the same thing as your underwear."

Rob's statement put a glow on Maureen's face. She smiled, but didn't say a word.

"What? Why're you looking at me like that?"

"You care, Rob. What you just said shows me that you care about me and that makes me feel good. I promise I won't pose for Jimmy." She planted a kiss on her finger and touched it to Rob's lips. "So, now that that's settled, what's going on in your life? Any new adventures to tell me about? Anything coming up?"

Silently, Rob contemplated Maureen's tanned features. He then brushed aside a strand of hair that had been hanging in front of her face. Finally, he answerd her question with a simple, "Got a flight down south next weekend. Nothing new, though."

"What about this coming Monday night. You have any plans yet? I'm off, you know."

Rob sat there, sitting very still, looking at Maureen, but not giving any sort of a reply. He had wanted her to bring up Monday night, and now that she had, he wasn't sure if he could go through with what he had to say.

It was Maureen who responded to her own question.

"I was thinking...maybe we could go see a movie or something? There's a couple of good ones playing in town."

This was it, Rob thought to himself. He had to go through with his strategy. And so, he did, but not before finishing off the Budweiser to ease his nerves. "Forget the movie," he answered awkwardly. "Let's drive down to Key West. We haven't done that in a while. I can pick you up after classes and we can be there in time for sunset at Mallory Dock."

"That sounds lovely."

"There's something else, too...about why I wanna take you there."

"What, Rob?"

"It's about us. About—" He stopped dead, going no further with his explanation.

"What about us?" Maureen pried, her thoughts racing, wanting to know what was on Rob's mind.

"Actually, it's about me. Personal kinds of things. Things that you don't know about. Things that have to do with my future...and maybe your future." Rob stopped again, this time taking in a deep breath of the bar's stale, smokey air. When he continued, all he said was, "It depends on you."

"What depends on me?"

"I can't tell you here. That's why I wanna go to Key West."

Maureen's chest was pounding with excitement. Deep in her heart, she felt for sure that Rob was hinting at marriage. Her two long years of waiting for him had finally paid off. Sensing Rob's uneasiness, though, she down-played the situation. "Okay, then. We'll drive down to Key West and talk there."

"When's your last class over?" Rob asked.

"It lets out at three-thirty. Is that too late?"

"Yeah."

"Well, I guess I can skip it if you want. How does one o'clock sound?"

"Better."

"Mo!" It was Jackie calling from behind the counter. The EuroAir mechanics were bombarding him with orders.

"Coming!" Maureen hugged Rob tightly, kissed him firmly on the mouth before he could stop her and was up and out of the booth in a flash.

Although a *NO GAMBLING* sign hung from the *Flight Deck's* rear wall, money changed hands at the bar's two pool tables on a nightly basis. Rob and his opponent were shooting eight ball. Two out of three games for fifty bucks. Nothing big stake-wise. Each man had one win, with the third game underway.

Rob was leaning against the wall, his hands vertically clutching a semi-warped cue stick in front of his body. He had his right leg bent at the knee so that his foot rested comfortably on the crossbar of a stool brought over for just that purpose. His eyes were sore from the heavy, smoke-tainted air that circulated about the bar. He watched in irritation as his opponent sank two solid-colored balls, with another about to drop into one of the side pockets.

Stacy, a thirty-eight year old divorcee, walked over to the back wall and sidled up next to Rob. Although she was a little on the plump side and not exactly bubbling over with intelligence, she was fun for an evening of pleasure—except that she talked too much. Brushing her arm against Rob, she whispered seductively, "You've got a nice stick, Rob. I like the way it curves naturally to the left." Stacy had been to bed with Rob on numerous occasions and had first-hand knowledge of his body's private attributes.

"Not now, Stacy," Rob said with annoyance. He knew what she wanted. It was all she ever wanted. But right now, all Rob wanted to do was concentrate on his shooting. A fuck would come later—and a blowjob. With Stacy, a blowjob was always guaranteed.

Rob opened his wallet and handed Stacy a twenty dollar bill. "Here," he said cooly. "Go buy a drink and bring me back a Bud." As Stacy waddled away, Rob tried easing her from his thoughts. It was difficult. Having not had sex in over a week, he needed relief badly. He finally managed to push her to the back of his mind when his opponent came up short on the next ball.

Rob slowly moved up to the table. He studied the various shots on the smooth green surface before settling on knocking the fourteen ball into the far corner pocket. He then sunk three more high-numbered balls before missing a shot. He resumed his stance against the wall.

Stacy strolled back and handed Rob his beer. "What'd I miss?" When Rob didn't respond, she asked, "Who's winning?"

"Even. This game decides it."

"And then what? Made up your mind yet, tush?"

"We'll go to your place."

"Only if you promise to buy me a bottle of Chablis on the way."

"Sure...whatever."

Rob's turn at the table came up again. He was facing a tough situation. He only had one shot—the striped twelve, which was partially blocked by the black eight ball. The shot was possible, but extreme care would be needed in its execution, plus a little "English" put on the cue ball.

Bracing himself across the pool table, Rob stretched

his body and took aim. One hand acted as a bridge, while the other clutched the stick. He struck the white cue ball lightly. He knew he'd blown it, though, when the cue ball pulled to the right, striking the eight ball. "Damn!" he exclaimed in dissatisfaction as he watched the eight ball fall into the side pocket, along with the game and fifty dollars.

"Nice shooting, Jensen," gloated Rob's opponent as he pocketed the cash.

"Tell me about it," Rob grunted. He put his arm around Stacy and guided her in the direction of the side door. As the two of them passed the cigarette machine, Rob stared over at Maureen, who was busy working behind the counter. When he saw Maureen staring back at him with a look of uncontrollable shock, Rob hurried Stacy toward the door.

Once outside, he wondered why Maureen had looked at him that way. She'd seen him leaving with Stacy before—and with other women. So why, tonight, did she look like death had called her name? Rob flexed his thoughts, then swept the mess away.

In the parking lot, Rob and Stacy met up with Nick and a group of his buddies. Rob could tell they had all been drinking heavily, especially Nick. He also sensed that something was up their sleeves.

"Hey, we're borrowin' a plane from 'Corrosion Corner' and goin' flyin'," Nick slurred, proving Rob's hunch correct. "You's guys wanna come?"

"We'll pass," Stacy stated firmly, answering for both of them without hesitation.

"S'at 'cause you're chicken or's 'cause Rob's taken care'f your wet pussy tonight?" Nick grinned, breaking out with a hard inebriated laugh.

Stacy furiously walked away from the group, going over and waiting by herself next to Rob's Blazer, which was parked at the far end of the lot.

"*Fat Slut!*" Nick yelled out. He laughed again, this time along with his buddies.

Before the group had settled down, Rob pulled Nick aside. "Are you crazy? You're too damned drunk to fly. Who's idea was this anyway?"

Nick pointed to himself. Another big grin was showing behind his thick beard.

"It's nothing to be smiling about, Nick. What if you crash? What about next Saturday?" Rob was thinking ahead about the run down to Colombia.

"What 'bout it?" Nick questioned without a care.

"Look, I can't stop you from making this flight tonight, but as your captain, I'm asking you not to go."

"Hey, man. I'm capt'n t'night. Not you."

Rob realized at this point that further persistence on his part was useless. Nick had already made up his stubborn mind to make an aerial joyride above Miami's glittering carpet of lights. Rob suspected that Nick, an addicted gambler, was dared into the risky venture. To find out for certain, he asked Nick, "How much you bet on this little stunt?"

"Five hunner'."

Five hundred dollars. At that price, Rob knew Nick wouldn't back down. "Don't kill yourself. I need a co-pilot on next weekend's run." Rob then turned away, leaving Nick standing there alone.

When Rob got to his blue Chevy truck, he unlocked the driver's door, climbed in and reached across to unlatch the passenger side. He flipped the handle for Stacy. After she got in, he asked, "Is your car here? 'Cause I don't plan on driving you back later to get it."

"No, it's at home. A friend dropped me off." And with that, Stacy reached across the center console and into Rob's lap, teasing him through his jeans.

Nick and his buddies piled into somebody's pick-up truck and drove to the northwest corner of the airport—"Corrosion Corner". They parked the vehicle on the grassy shoulder alongside Northwest 67th Avenue, then ran across the road. After hopping a chain-link fence, the men ran through a maze of tramp airfreighters.

One of the pilots in the group—not Nick—suggested, "Let's take up Romeo-Charlie." All agreed that N23RC was a good choice. And so, they moved briskly across the oily ramp to where the dull, metallic Curtiss C-46 was chocked. N23RC was a bulky, twin-engined taildragger leased by Trans-Carib Aero, a Miami-based company in the business of transporting poultry out to the Caribbean for the hotel industry there.

Nick was especially familiar with the aircraft. He had flown the plane on numerous occasions for Trans-Carib Aero before being hired by Falcon—but always as copilot. Tonight he had the chance to captain N23RC—to feel the power of authority that the left-seat brought. Not since the crash down in Brazil had Nick flown left-seat.

Nick had been drinking the morning of that bloody crash, but not to any extreme. The aircraft was a modified Beechcraft D-18S with bombay doors and a fuselage holding tank. Nick was flying in an area approximately 250 miles northwest of Rio de Janeiro under contract from the Brazilian government. His piloting mission was to stock the Furnas Reservoir with fish hatchlings.

After several low altitude passes downstream from the Furna Dam, the aircraft's elevator control cable had snapped, causing Nick to lose all pitch control of the Beech-18. It hadn't even been his fault. A control cable breakage was such a rare and deadly occurrence, that even a totally sober pilot wouldn't have had a chance at safely maneuvering the aircraft.

Nick's heart had pounded almost fatally as he fought the control wheel in the cockpit, trying to regain control of the aircraft as the plane drew nearer to the trees lining the bank of the large reservoir. But Nick's futile attempt ended in a grisly mess. His unconscious body had remained trapped inside the pile of freshly corrugated aluminum for several hours before he was freed by a rescue crew. By then, his foot could not be saved.

Nick's intoxicated state had had nothing to do with the downing of the aircraft. The crash had been mechanically induced. Yet, because the toxicology reports from the hospital showed alcohol in his bloodstream, the accident was officially listed as pilot induced—"Flying Under The Influence". After a year of rehabilitation in Brazil, Nick had made his way north to Miami, where he quickly found a new life copiloting the derelicts out of "Corrosion Corner".

No preflight check was performed on N23RC. With the wheel chocks removed and both cargo doors swung open, Nick and his buddies climbed the ladder and crawled into the cavernous belly of the C-46. A short time later, the engines coughed and belched angrily as if in protest before finally turning over to a steady beat. Soon, N23RC was taxiing out into the night.

CHAPTER FIVE

Sunday morning

At quarter past two in the morning, the lights above the *Flight Deck's* pool tables were out. The last customer had left shortly after the bar's two o'clock closing time, leaving Jackie and Maureen alone in the tavern. There was plenty of work to be done by both of them. Cigarette butts were scattered about on the dirty floor. At least fifty glasses needed washing. The bar stools had to be overturned and placed on top of the counter. It was going to be a late morning.

While scooping a small accumulation of butts into a dust pan, Maureen broke down and began to cry. She dropped the pan and its contents and sat down on the cold, vinyl floor. Tonight had been emotionally too much for her. She needed so badly to ease the throbbing pain in her heart. She couldn't grasp reality. She couldn't comprehend why Rob had left with Stacy. Was there something physically unattractive about herself that Rob didn't like? Maureen was confused.

Jackie came over and sat down beside Maureen. "You want to talk about it, Mo?" he asked tenderly.

Trying to hold back her flow of tears, she sniffled a few times, swallowed hard and then said, "It's Rob. I don't know what to think about my relationship with him anymore. He hurt me so bad tonight when he—" Maureen stopped in midsentence. "I mean, it always hurt a little when he left with other women, but not as much as it did tonight. Tonight I felt cheated on for the first time. I felt so low, Jackie. So used."

"It's alright for you to have those feelings, Mo. I understand what you're going through."

Maureen continued, "It's as if Rob wants me to be there for him when he needs me. But then when I need him, he's not there. It's like I have to stand in line behind all those sluts he sleeps with. It hurts, Jackie. It hurts bad. I just don't know what to think anymore."

"Mo, let me tell you something about Rob. What he does on the surface has no bearing on what he actually feels inside. What I'm trying to say is that there are some people in this world who just can't cope with their emotions. Rob's one of them. It's because of his past. Once, a couple of years back, he started opening up to me, telling me about what had happened to him. But before I could get the whole story, he froze up. It was as if he couldn't face up to himself. That's why he hides what he really feels." Jackie noticed Maureen gazing at him quizzically. "Am I making any sense? You look puzzled."

"It's just that sometimes Rob really seems to care about me. Like tonight when he asked me to go down to the Keys with him. I really thought he was going to ask me to marry him. But now...I don't know."

"Well, if you want my two cents worth, Rob *does* care about you. He may even *love* you, for all I know."

"Why are you so sure? You saw him leave with Stacy."

Jackie thought for a moment. "Why am I sure? I'll tell you why," he said with a serious look on his face. Then, very fatherly, he put his arms around Maureen and gently rested her head upon his shoulder. "Men are funny, Mo. They've got this gratification urge buried deep within their loins that has to be satisfied. What Rob is doing is perfectly natural and healthy. But don't get me wrong. I'm not siding with him. He *could* go about his personal business a little more discreetly."

Jackie made a slight coughing sound to clear a drip in his throat. "What I'm getting at is this, Mo. Those sexual encounters of Rob's are *not* special to him. The moments he enjoys most are those spent with you. Long walks on the beach, country drives, going to the movies or out for a meal. Don't you see? Those are things he shares only with you. He treasures those moments. If he slept with you, you'd become just another whore to him. He doesn't want that. I don't think you do either." Jackie gave Maureen a soft kiss on the forehead, then released her from his arms. "Be patient, Mo. One day things will fall into place."

Maureen wiped her eyes dry with the bottom of her blouse. She was feeling a touch better from what Jackie had told her, but she still had many unanswered questions floating around in her head. Was it possible Rob was trying to face up to his feelings? Was that why he wanted to take her to Key West? And if so, why did he leave with Stacy? Were his sexual needs so great that he couldn't hold out for two more nights? Maureen wondered how Monday was going to fair for herself. She wondered hard.

The quilt covers had long been pushed aside as Stacy lay naked, her head resting peacefully on Rob's muscular chest. A candle glowed atop an antique dresser, giving off the only light in the shabby Hialeah apartment. Mutton, an oversized beagle, was curled up at the foot of the bed.

The dog had slept through the erotic sounds that had filled the bedroom over the past several hours.

Fondling the thick, 18K gold chain encircling Rob's neck, Stacy asked, "You know why I like making it with you?" Although she knew Rob didn't care, she told him anyway. "It's because you wait for me to explode before letting yourself go. Barry never did that. He'd just hurry up and shoot his load. It'd take him all of five minutes. Ten if I was lucky. Then he'd get up and leave me to grab a beer from the fridge. No foreplay. No afterplay. Sex was a real drag with Barry."

"How come you tell me about your husband every time I fuck you?"

"Ex-husband."

"Whatever, Stacy. I'm tired of hearing about him...about what he did and didn't do to you." Rob had nothing in common with Stacy. They had nothing to talk about. To him, she was just another piece of willing female flesh sprawled out on a bed. He leaned towards the night-table to catch a look at the clock. "Damn! Gotta go," he told her as he sprung his body upright in bed.

"Why?"

"'Cause it's almost four o'clock. The bass are waiting."

But Stacy had other ideas. Easing Rob back down onto the crumpled sheets, she seductively whispered in his ear, "You can't leave yet. I haven't had dessert." Using the long, polished fingernail of her middle finger, she delicately traced a line from Rob's lips down to his pelvic region. Then, positioning her hand between his legs, Stacy softly massaged Rob's tenderness, teasing him with each stroke. When she felt him grow hard, her moist lips replaced her fingers. Long strands of black hair brushed against Rob's thighs as Stacy's head passionately worked up and down in an even rhythm. She took all of him in.

Then, as Rob filled her mouth with warmth, she swallowed—twice.

Reaching across the king-sized bed, Stacy grabbed the bottle of Chablis off the nightstand. She drank a bit of the white wine, altering the taste lingering in her throat, then offered the bottle to Rob.

He accepted, leaned forward while bringing the bottle to his mouth, then emptied it. Totally drained and exhausted, Rob rested his tired body against the bed's headboard.

Stacy cuddled up close. Again, she became transfixed on Rob's gold chain. Attached to the shimmering piece of jewelry was a black bird, its wings stretched out in flight profile. Clutched in the bird's claws was a single leaf. The curious combination looked beautiful in the flickering candlelight. "What kind of bird is this, Rob?" she asked, playing with the charm.

"A falcon."

"It's different. I've never seen anything like it in a store. Where'd you buy it?"

"I didn't. The guy I fly for had a bunch of them made up for all of his people. We're suppose to wear them all the time as, you know...some sort of sign of unity or something."

"Then how come I never saw it on you before?"

"'Cause I don't always wear the fucking thing. That's why. The only reason I'm wearing it now is 'cause I forgot to take it off when I got home from the test-flight I made yesterday morning."

"Oh." Stacy's attention focused in on the leaf. She thought it appeared odd with its seven finger-like leaflets radiating outward from the center stem. Prying, she asked, "Does this leaf mean anything?"

Although Rob was relieved that Stacy's naivety didn't allow her to recognize the leaf as a marijuana leaf, he still didn't like the direction her questioning was heading. "Damn, woman!" he stated boldly. "You sure ask some dumb things. It's just a fucking leaf." Rob decided right then and there that he'd had enough of Stacy. Without even saying good-bye, he rose out of bed, threw on his clothes and walked to the front door.

Stacy called out to him, "Don't forget to turn the lock before—"

"Lock your own damn door," Rob muttered under his breath as he slammed the door shut, not caring that his action probably rattled the picture frames hanging from the cheap stucco walls inside Stacy's apartment. He quickly got into his Blazer and headed for home to hook up to his boat trailer.

While stopped at a red light on LeJeune Road, Rob's mind became active. His thoughts were mainly about bass fishing in the Everglades until he remembered about the airfreighter's oil leak problem. Actually, Rob didn't have much to think about in regards to the DC-4's number two engine. George had promised him he'd fix the problem by the end of the week. A week gave George plenty of time, Rob reasoned. Plenty of time to ready the airfreighter for the long flight to Colombia.

George arrived at Opa Locka Airport rather early for a Sunday morning—just shortly after sunrise to be exact. After unloading a cumbersome tool chest from the rear of his work van, he poured himself a cup of steaming, black coffee from a half-gallon thermos jug. Sipping the coffee slowly, he proceeded to plan out his strategy for the airfreighter.

When the styrofoam cup was empty, George leisurely made his way toward a section of iron scaffolding. He rolled the metal platform underneath the airfreighter's number two engine, where he would be spending the better part of an hour checking for oil deposits in each of the fourteen cylinders on the Pratt and Whitney R-2000 Twin Wasp powerplant. He brought his tool chest over and climbed the platform.

Since the engine cowling did not require removal to pull the front set of plugs from the twin rows of cylinders, George decided to work on them first. Starting with the outer row, he one-by-one loosened the spark plugs from their seats. No unusual accumulations of oil were found. He then repeated the process on the inner row of cylinders. The culprit was finally discovered when he pulled the plug from the number seven cylinder head. As he removed the spark plug, a stream of black, gunky lubricant poured out, coating his arm with its slickness.

Next, George needed to remove the second plug from the number seven cylinder, but to do so, he had to first detach the three-piece aluminum cowling encasing the powerful, air-cooled engine. George knew the task would be easier with the help of a second man, but that was a luxury he didn't have.

While unfastening one of the flanged clips on the bottom cowling section, George accidentally tore a sizable gash in his right thumb. The blood oozed endlessly from the flesh wound. As the pain traveled up his arm, George spat out a series of cuss words into the morning air. Nobody was around to hear him. George blamed the aircraft for his injury as if the plane was human—as if the silent DC-4 was a vixenish female taking revenge on him for undressing her in broad daylight. Such was the way with aircraft.

Subsequent to wrapping a filthy shop rag tightly around his hemorrhaging finger, George went back to parting the cowling from the engine, lowering its three bulky pieces to the ground without care. He turned back to the engine, where he had his work cut out for him. Of the fourteen cylinders that could have gone bad, the number seven was the most dreaded by George, for it was connected to the oil sump return system. One more thing to get in his way.

After removing the second plug from the number seven cylinder and wiping off the oil and grime, George decided it was time for his second coffee break of the morning. He climbed down from the scaffolding and walked over to the van. Opening the side panel door, he sat down on the vehicle's floorboard, where a jumble of bolts, spare parts and rags were scattered about in no particular order. For George, the only organized way to work was in a disorganized environment. Neatly arranged shelves of inventory in a fully-stocked parts warehouse was not his idea of a good work setting—whereas, working out of a cluttered van was like heaven.

George twisted the top off the thermos and drank the coffee straight from the jug, not bothering to use one of the dirty styrofoam cups lying about in his van. As he swallowed the hot liquid, he watched with amusement as a student pilot struggled to keep his wings level after lifting off from the runway in a single-engine Cessna 152. The turbulence coming over the pine trees on the north side of Runway 9L was a constant menace to neophyte flyers at Opa Locka Airport.

George knew from first-hand experience. He'd gone through the same learning process only a few short years ago when he took his first flying lesson at Opa Locka. Flying was a skill George had wanted to master since his days as an Air Force mechanic in Vietnam. But it wasn't until he'd started turning wrenches for Falcon's organization that he managed to afford the luxury of earning a Private Pilot Certificate.

George closed his eyes and fell into a daydream

about his Long-Eze, the rear-engined kitplane he'd spent nearly two years putting together in his garage. It was a strange sort of an aircraft—different from most conventional planes in that its main wing extended outward from the rear of the fuselage, while its much smaller canard wing protruded from the nose. Together, both sets of wings provided a stable platform in which to roam the skies.

The Long-Eze was George's pride. His favorite hours aloft were those spent cruising above South Florida's beaches, waving his wings at the girls, especially over Virginia Key, a spot frequented by nude sunbathers.

Still dreaming about his airplane, George cleared a path on the van's littered floorboard and layed himself down. Within seconds, he had drifted off into a deep sleep. The airfreighter was not touched by George the rest of the day.

CHAPTER SIX

Monday afternoon

Rob usually enjoyed driving through the Florida Keys with Maureen, sometimes stopping for a drink with her at one of the many rustic bars dotting A1A. He usually enjoyed the breathtaking panorama of natural blues, greens and turquoises of the water while crossing each of the forty-two bridges on the ride down to Key West. He usually enjoyed these things, but not today.

Something was wrong with Maureen and Rob sensed it. Maybe it was the way he'd caught her staring blankly at him several times. Maybe it was how she was sitting—sort of sideways on the front seat, leaning back against the locked passenger door. She never sat like that. And she hadn't said a word to him the entire trip—not since he'd picked her up from campus earlier in the afternoon and she had said, "Hi."

Rob had tried ignoring the situation up until now by listening to the radio, but at mile marker 53 on U.S. Highway One, the music turned into static. Rob immediately went for the dial, trying to tune in a decent FM station. His effort was worthless. The further away from Miami he drove, the more station fade he experienced. Pointing to the back seat of the Blazer, he asked Maureen, "You wanna reach back there and grab the cassette case for me?"

Maureen leaned over the seat and retrieved the box of tapes. Still not saying a word to Rob, she placed the case on his lap.

"Thanks." Rob waited for a response from Maureen, although he wasn't sure what kind of a response he was waiting for. Perhaps something that showed she would communicate with him, he thought. Any kind of a sign would do. Anything was better than nothing. But nothing was what he got. Having had enough of the afternoon the way it was going, Rob chose to finally do something about it.

Looking into the rear-view mirror to see if anyone was tailgating him and seeing that there wasn't, he pulled the Blazer off to the side of the road at the entrance to the Seven Mile Bridge. He turned off the ignition, then looked over at Maureen. He looked right into her blue eyes.

The stare he got back frightened him. It was as if Maureen was looking straight through him—almost as if he didn't exist. But he did exist. He knew he wasn't dreaming. He knew he wasn't having a nightmare. Everything was real. Hesitantly, he asked, "Is something the matter?"

"Oh, you've noticed?" It was a stern remark from Maureen, but there was care etched into the curves of her face.

"I haven't noticed anything except that you're acting strange. That's why I asked...'cause you were staring right at me...but off into space at the same time. It's like I've done something that really pissed you off, but I don't know what."

"You've changed, Rob. Something's bothering you deep down inside and it's changed you. You haven't been yourself ever since you picked me up from school this afternoon."

"Me...I'm different? What the hell's going on here?" Rob was puzzled beyond belief. He had no idea what Maureen was talking about. She was the one who was different. Not him. "I don't get it. Is this some kind of a joke?"

Maureen gave Rob the same blank expression, only this time it was longer. Finally, she answered, "No. This is no joke. You've changed."

"But I'm me, Maureen. These jeans are me!" Rob exclaimed, slapping his hands on his best pair of faded denims. "This T-shirt is me! This truck is me! How the hell can you say I'm different? I wanna know, so tell me. How?"

"I don't know exactly." Maureen looked down at her lap. "Maybe it's not you. Maybe it is me," she said softly.

"You're damn right it's you...'cause it sure as hell isn't me."

Maureen closed her eyes. "I think I'm still upset over you and Stacy leaving together the other night at the bar. It was the way you looked at me and then quickly turned away. That hurt."

Rob became defensive. "Why should that bother you? You've seen me leave with her before. Lots of times." Then, looking out the Chevy's windshield, he muttered under his breath, "She's only a fuck anyway. That's all."

"Robert, don't speak like that in front of me!"

"Hey, I'm sorry, okay? But it's the truth. There's nothing between me and Stacy. *Nothing!*"

Maureen unlocked the door, opened it and jumped out of the Blazer. She spun around, grabbed her purse off the seat and stomped over to the bridge's guard rail, about thirty feet away. Sitting down on the metal railing, she began to cry. Her eyes reddened, but remained completely dry. She had no more tears to spill.

Rob exited out the driver's side and paced over to Maureen. He leaned down in front of her. He tried getting her to look at him, but she wouldn't.

Just then, a Florida Highway patrolman pulled off the roadway, parked his black and yellow Mustang behind Rob's Blazer and flashed on his blue roof lights. The patrolman stepped out of his car. Walking over to where Rob and Maureen were, he dipped his wide-rimmed hat and inquired, "Is there a problem, ma'am?"

It was Rob who answered. "The only problem here is you butting into our business."

The trooper didn't appreciate Rob's remark. He grabbed his nightstick and poked Rob in the gut with a brutal jab. "I asked the lady a question and I ain't leavin' 'til I get an honest answer outta her. So you keep your fuckin', bad-ass mouth closed." The highway patrolman then repeated his question to Maureen. "Is there a problem, ma'am?"

Maureen still said nothing.

"Ma'am, is this bad-ass interferin' with you or tryin' to cause you harm in any manner or form?"

Rob spoke up again, this time to Maureen. "You don't have to answer him if you don't want to, Maureen. He's got no right harassing you like this. Let's just get back in the truck and get going, okay?"

Again the trooper dug his stick into Rob's gut. "Listen, boy! I'm goin' to run your bad-ass in if you make just one more utterance with that smart-ass mouth of yours. Do you understand me, boy?"

With his stomach throbbing in pain, Rob understood quite clearly. If there was one thing he didn't want, it was getting thrown in jail. He shook his head several times, acknowledging the trooper's warning, wishing to hell that Florida's highway patrolmen would keep to the major expressways. Their attitudes were just too cocky for the Keys.

The trooper asked Maureen for the fourth time, "Is there some kind of a problem goin' on here, ma'am? Anythin' I can help you with? An escort perhaps?"

"No, officer. There's no problem. I'm just tired...that's all."

"Jus' checkin', ma'am. Never can tell what kind of shit you find drivin' these big, four-wheel drive vehicles. Jus' never can tell." The trooper then asked to see Rob's license. He walked to his car and called in the license on the radio, checking for any outstanding warrants. When Rob's record checked out clean, he handed the license back to Rob, got in his car and drove off heading north.

Maureen looked into Rob's eyes. She was no longer crying. "Don't you see, Rob? You *have* changed. You've never talked back to a policeman before. *Never!* It's not like you to do something that foolish. He was going to put you in jail."

"Screw him. He's just a state-bred pig trying to play cop."

"There you go again. Why are you talking like this? What's happening to you? Where's the sweet guy I used to know? The guy I love?"

"Maureen, I—" Rob stopped short.

"Yes?"

"Shit, I don't know. I don't know anything anymore. It's like—" He cut himself off again, then walked back to the truck, his mind slipping into a mild state of depression. "You coming, Maureen?"

She rose to her feet and slowly walked toward the Blazer, shaking her head in curiosity as to Rob's odd behavior. Before climbing into the truck, she looked across at Rob with the most serious expression she had ever worn on her face. "Robert, I think I know you better than you know yourself. I can sense that there's something happening in your life. Something you're not telling me. Something terrible. I don't know what it is, but it's big and it's eating you to pieces and I wish you'd open up and tell me about it so we can work it out together...because it's affecting both of us, Robert. You know I'd do anything in the world for you. That's because I love you so much. The last thing I want to see is for you to get hurt. I'm praying for you, Robert. I want you to know that. I'm praying that someday you'll figure out what it is you want out of life and that once you do decide, that I'll still be a part of it." With her sermon over, Maureen stepped up into the Blazer and fastened her seatbelt. Looking straight ahead, she said, "Now, let's just go to Key West and have a good time."

If a good time was what Maureen wanted, then a good time was what she'd get—that is, if Rob could break out of his depression. He started the Chevy's engine, pulled out onto the road and then onto the Seven Mile Bridge. He didn't bother with the cassettes, choosing instead to listen to the radio's static, wondering silently how the situation had gotten turned around. All afternoon, it had been Maureen who was the quiet one. Now, in a matter of minutes, she had managed to make him the outcast.

The more Rob thought, the more despondent he became until, finally, his thoughts turned to his escape plan. He wondered if he'd actually be able to pull off the maneuver without getting caught up in Falcon's far-reaching claws. He wondered, too, whether Maureen would be accompanying him on the escape. He hoped he would find enough courage by the end of the night to ask her to go with him. He wasn't so sure now.

Midway across the bridge, with three and a half

miles still to go before reaching Little Duck Key, Rob started thinking back on how he'd first gotten involved with Falcon's organization. He blamed it partially on the major airlines. It was the only rationalization he could come up with. If the airlines hadn't consistently refused him employment, he never would have accepted Gustavo's offer to make one drug run and then be "free-to-go-as-he-pleased", which turned out to be nothing but a jaded lie anyhow.

But because the high-paying airlines had never hired him and because he had been tired of flying for the "Corrosion Corner" airfreight haulers, Rob had accepted Gustavo's offer. He had accepted it, though, under one condition—that he be allowed to choose his own copilot. Someone with low-altitude flying experience. Someone with balls. Someone who would jump at the chance to make big money. Nick Donovan. For all the bad Rob had seen in the man, he had always known Nick to be a damn good pilot. Naturally, Nick had jumped at the offer—for the money, of course.

And the money *was* there for each of them. But for Rob, flying for a doper operation hadn't turned out like he'd expected. What had seemed like easy money, turned out to be a living hell—full of anguish, fear and near-lethal nightmares. Like countless pilots before him, he had been suckered into the drug world. He had learned the hard way that smuggling was a fool's game. A deadly game not to be reckoned with.

CHAPTER SEVEN

Monday Night
   Rob guessed he had shown Maureen a good enough time at the Mallory Dock "sunset party", but he couldn't be sure because she hadn't said so. He was surprised that she had held his hand as they walked among the street people and other revelers at Key West's nightly celebration of the downing of the sun.
   They had strolled for two hours along the concrete seawall, watching the action together. There'd been a pair of jugglers twirling flaming torches back and forth to each other. Another death-defying act had been performed by a pony-tailed tight-rope walker. Several street musicians played songs for spare change. The flutist had been particularly good, especially when he'd played the *Jethro Tull* tunes. There'd been a lady hawking freshly-baked cookies. Rob had bought a large chocolate chip cookie for himself and a peanut butter chip for Maureen. He had also purchased a green bird made out of a palm frond by one of the local craftsmen and had given it to Maureen as a peace offering. He didn't know if she liked it or not. She never said so either way.
   Anyhow, if Maureen hadn't enjoyed herself at the "sunset party", at least she'd have a good time at the

Schooner Inn Tavern, a sort of nautical motif, hole-in-the-wall bar off of Duval Street. As Rob and Maureen squeezed their way through the mostly young crowd inside the "salty" tavern, their ears quickly adjusted to the conversation and live music echoing off the walls in loud reverberations.

The air inside the bar as hot, stale and muggy and despite the fact that the side doors were opened wide onto the street and despite the efforts of the overhead ceiling fans to circulate the air, most everybody in the joint was perspiring. But that was life at the *Schooner Inn* and nobody seemed to mind.

Rob guided Maureen through the maze of people until they were standing just to the left of the stage, inches away from a conglomerate of speakers blaring with rock music. Rob turned around, looking for an empty table. He didn't see one, but spotted two empty chairs at an occupied table. "Wait here," he told Maureen. "I'm gonna see if I can snatch those chairs for us. I don't feel like standing here all night."

Rob walked over to the table, where a young woman of about twenty-three years of age was sitting with two sailors dressed in French naval uniforms. Rob figured the sailors were off the French destroyer tied up alongside the Key West naval yard. It was obvious to Rob that the three at the table were having a difficult time conversing, since the two Frenchmen appeared to speak no English, while the American girl spoke no French. "Anybody using these two seats?" Rob asked the girl.

"No. You can have them."

"Thanks." Rob signaled to Maureen with his hands. As he waited for her to weave her way through the thick mass of bodies moving about on the dance floor, he pulled out her chair. When she sat down, he pushed her in closer to the table, then sat down himself. "You want a drink?"

"Yes, please," Maureen answered, almost in a daze. "I'll have a vodka and tonic with a twist of lime." She was still in awe of the way Rob helped her into her seat. He'd never done anything like that before. Maybe her talk to him in Marathon had sunk into his head, she thought.

"Okay, vodka and tonic with lime," Rob confirmed as he got up to go over to the bar. "I'll be right back."

It was more than ten minutes before Rob came back from the bar with drinks and coasters in hand—a vodka and tonic for Maureen and a Budweiser for himself. He sat down and immediately noticed that the young woman seated at the table was still struggling over the same conversation with her two foreign friends. It appeard to Rob that she was trying to describe some sort of animal using hand gestures and sounds to get her message understood. Her method wasn't working.

Finally, in exasperation, the girl turned to Rob and Maureen. "Either of you speak French?"

Rob answered with a brisk, "No."

Maureen didn't give a reply, but shook her head that she didn't.

"I just thought you might," said the girl. She then turned her attention back to the Frenchmen, determined to get her point across.

"What're you describing?" Rob asked curiously, breaking into the girl's futile attempt at explaining whatever it was she was explaining.

"About alligators. I'm down on vacation from up north and went to the Everglades the other day. They had these airboat rides out there and I took one and saw real live alligators for the first time in my life. It was really exciting. I just wanted to know if these guys have ever seen alligators...'cause if not, I'd like to drive them up to go see some. Do you know if there's alligators in France?"

"I'm not sure," answered Rob, "but I know how to find out. You got a pen?"

She didn't.

Rob turned to Maureen. "You got a pen in your purse?" he asked, knowing she carried just about everything in her purse.

Maureen shuffled through the pounds of junk stored in her cloth bag until she came up with a black, felt-tipped marker. She gave the marker to Rob, wondering what he was going to use if for, but mostly wondering why he was suddenly paying more attention to the other woman at the table than he was to her.

With the felt marker, Rob quickly drew a crude sketch of an alligator on a paper napkin. When he finished with the picture, he passed the napkin across to the two sailors.

"*Ah, qui!*" they ackowledged, shaking their heads. The Frenchmen did indeed know what alligators were. Whether or not there were alligators in France—that question was left up in the air.

"That was great," said the vacationing girl, amazed how Rob had broken the language barrier using only a simple cartoon drawing. "I've been sitting here for half an hour making a fool of myself trying to get these guys to understand me and all you did was show them a picture. That was really great!"

"I travel out of the country a lot," Rob explained. "I'm a pilot."

"Then you have experience at this kind of stuff," she stated plainly.

"Some," Rob interjected as he eyed the shapely figure of a curly-haired brunette walking past the table on her way to the restroom in the back corner of the bar. Out the corner of his left eye, Rob also noticed Maureen watching him watch the brunette. He brushed it off as nothing to worry about. When the girl finally disappeared into the restroom, Rob again turned to the young woman sitting at the table and asked, "Do you even know these guys' names?"

"No...but I've been calling the short, puggy one *Red Wine*," she said, pointing to the Frenchman sitting directly across from Rob, "'cause that's all he can say in English. I think he keeps inviting me back to his ship for a drink with him, but I'm not sure."

Rob laughed.

So did the two Frenchmen, both displaying big grins on their faces. They knew they were being talked about and enjoyed being the focus of attention.

Rob and the vacationing girl continued discussing the Frenchmen for a while longer, with Rob totally ignoring Maureen, but not on purpose. Then, when the girl boldly asked Rob to dance, Rob turned to Maureen and asked, "You wouldn't mind, would you? It's only a dance."

Picking up her vodka and tonic, Maureen splashed the drink into Rob's face, then grabbed her purse and stormed towards the ladies restroom, where she passed the curly-haired brunette in the doorway.

Maureen looked at herself in the restroom mirror after having sat and cried in a stall for fifteen minutes. What she saw was a pretty face accented with just the right touch of cosmetics, making her blue eyes look almost cat-like—except that her eyes were spilling over with new-found tears and she didn't feel very pretty. Streaks of mascara were already marking her cheeks. What she *did* feel was loneliness and hurt. How could Rob have done such a thing to her? How could he have made her feel so ugly and worthless?

Oddly enough, Maureen still felt a deep love for Rob. She still wanted him. She just didn't know what to do about him anymore. Wiping the tears from her eyes with a paper towel, she thought about the reason Rob had brought her down to Key West in the first place—to discuss their future, which he still hadn't done. She also thought about the discussion she'd had with Jackie on Saturday night. What was it Jackie had said about Rob—something about manly urges? Was that why Rob had felt the compulsion to dance with the vacationing girl? A girl he didn't even know? Was that why he had followed the curly-haired brunette with his eyes all the way to the ladies room? Was Rob just satisfying his inner maleness?

Maureen tried reasoning with herself. She tried figuring Rob out. She tried coming up with an answer as to why Rob wouldn't express his urges with her, if Jackie's "manly urge" theory was indeed the problem.

Maureen's crying had caused her sinuses to fill. Pulling another paper towel out of the dispenser, she blew her nose. Then, to refreshen herself, she washed the running make-up from her face. While washing, an answer came to her. She towel dried her face and again looked at herself in the mirror. This time, she seemed brighter. At least now she had a positive direction in which to go forward.

Her solution was to shock Rob into reality. Cause him to battle his past. Force him to confront his feelings—to admit his love for her. Never before had she been forceful with Rob. Jackie had always hinted to her to be patient. But patience hadn't worked.

Feeling strong and full of renewed self-confidence, Maureen reapplied her make-up. After checking her lipstick once more in the mirror, she left the privacy of the ladies room and walked back to the table. She took notice that Rob was still seated there, as was the vacationing girl and her two sailor friends.

The irony of the situation hit Maureen when she realized the band was no longer playing on the stage. They had ended their set while she was in the restroom. Instead, MTV was being broadcast on a large television screen hung from the side wall. Maureen laughed inside, knowing that Rob hadn't even gotten his chance to dance with the girl.

Taking her place at the table, Maureen sat quietly for a moment, allowing her calmness to soak in. Then, when she was positive she was ready to begin her act—and that's exactly what it was going to be, an act—she released her ploy upon Rob.

She called out for his undivided attention and when she got it, she stated earnestly, "I want you to be truthful with me, Robert. I want you to think real hard and tell me to my face whether or not you hold even the slightest trace of love for me. I can wait a few minutes for an answer, but not too long because I've already wasted too much time not knowing where I stand with you. I deserve to know, Robert. I deserve to know whether or not you love me."

Rob felt as if he was pegged up against a piece of plywood embedded with a thousand rusty nails. He wanted to say yes. He was going to say yes. But after waiting nearly two full minutes before answering, he lied and said, "No." It was the first time he'd ever actually lied to Maureen. Up until now, he had never told her that he didn't love her. He'd just never told her that he did. His stomach felt queasy. He thought he was going to be sick.

Maureen wasn't surprised by Rob's response. It was what she'd expected out of him. She retorted with an accusation. "You're lying, Robert. I know you are. I just don't know why. Maybe it's because I've been too good to you. Well, that's all changing as of this moment. From now on, you're going to experience what life's like without me. You're going to see what it's like not having somebody who's caring to fall back on whenever things get tough. You're going to realize you've made a big mistake, Robert."

But Rob hadn't caught a word of what she had said. He was transfixed in his own little world. His mind was in a daze, spinning at a horrendous rate, trying to figure out why he couldn't bring himself to admit his love. It was the same haunting question coming back to terrorize him. Why?

When Maureen realized Rob hadn't heard her, she got up from her seat and walked over to the bar, where the band's female vocalist was ordering a drink. The two women casually exchanged words. Maureen then came back to the table and waited in silence for the band to return to the stage for their next set. It was the longest twelve minutes of Maureen's life.

The tuning of an electric guitar on stage was Maureen's signal to begin the finale of her act. She reached for Rob's clammy hands and forcefully pronounced, "Come, Robert. I want one dance with you before I go." When Rob protested, Maureen asserted herself, "Don't give me a hard time. I deserve *at least* this much from you."

She grasped his hands tightly and pulled him out of his chair. Together, they walked onto the dance floor. Maureen was oblivious to the crowd of people in the tavern staring at her and Rob. She turned toward the stage, indicating to the female singer that she'd be ready in a minute.

Then, turning back to Rob, Maureen said in her softest voice, "When the music starts, I want you to listen carefully to the words...especially to the last verse. Let them sink into your head, Robert. If you don't, then someday you'll be very sorry because you're going to wake up one cold morning and you're going to run your tired hands through your hair, which by then will be gray, and you're going to suddenly realize that you're an old man and that your whole life has somehow slipped by you. And when the lonely chill of the air clutches your body beneath the covers and you roll over to cuddle up to somebody warm, that somebody's not going to be there. Your bed will be empty. Not because your lover got up to get a drink of water or to use the bathroom. But because she was never there to begin with. Because you never let her in. And *that*, Robert, is when you're finally going to realize that your life has been a waste. An illusion. Because *love*, Robert...love is what life is all about! Love and sharing." Maureen wrapped her arms around Rob and drew him close against her breasts. Her heart pumped nervously, achingly.

The speakers crackled. It was the voice of the band's female vocalist. "We have a special request tonight to play '*Desperado*' by the *Eagles*. This song goes out to Rob from Maureen. We hope you all enjoy our version of this sentimental rock ballad."

As the music began drifting out over the bar's speaker system, Maureen led Rob in a loving slow dance. One-by-one, other couples joined them on the dance floor, swaying gently to the words and the music.

The song told about emotional barriers, about love, about Rob's future if he didn't face up to his feelings. The song made Maureen cry on Rob's shoulder.

When the ballad was over, Maureen released the hold she had on Rob. She said to him, "If you ever need to talk, you can still come see me at Jackie's place. But after tonight...our relationship is finished." Tears billowed down her cheeks as she turned away from Rob. "Take care of yourself," she whispered, walking away, leaving him standing there alone on the dance floor surrounded by the other couples. After making her way back to the table, Maureen picked up her purse and headed for the front door.

Rob chased after her. He caught her arm just as she was exiting the bar. "Where're you going?"

"I'm checking into a motel for the night. I'll take a Greyhound back to Miami in the morning. I've got money."

"But, Maureen—"

"Good-bye, Robert." She kissed him on the lips and hurried away, losing herself in the crowd of people on the sidewalk, hoping her ploy had served its purpose, hoping her act would bring Rob to his senses.

Rob sat alone on the edge of the concrete seawall at Mallory Dock. He hated himself and he hated everything he had ever done to hurt Maureen. He felt like jumping off the seawall into the darkened water and swimming out into the harbor until his muscles were void of all their strength and then letting his body sink to the water's depths. But, as always, he found reason not to carry out his suicide.

For the rest of the night and most of Tuesday morning, Rob sat on the hard-surfaced seawall, not moving from his spot. Although his body remained motionless, his mind was a labyrinth of activity—his thoughts switching from this to that, then shooting back around to something he'd thought about hours before and then on again to something totally new. He never focused on any one thing—not until his brain conjured up an image of a letter.

A letter! That was it! That was the solution to his problem! He could write Maureen a letter. That way, he could explain everything to her without ever having to face her in person again. He could explain about his fucked up life. He could explain about his misapplied flying career and about Falcon and about his escape plan. He could explain to Maureen about how he had wanted so badly to ask her to come with him on his escape. But most of all, he could use the letter to explain his true feelings for her. He could tell her about his love for her. And because he could hold off mailing the letter until late Friday, he could guarantee himself that Maureen wouldn't get it until the following week. By that time, he'd be well into his escape—long gone from Florida. Long gone from Maureen.

Satisfied with his idea about the letter, Rob got up from the seawall and walked over to the lot where his truck was parked. Within minutes, he was heading north on A1A, his suicidal thoughts once again flushed away to the back of his mind.

CHAPTER EIGHT

Friday morning

From the looks of the dilapidated room, its dirtied and splintered wood flooring, plumbing that led nowhere and several torn mattresses strewn about, Maureen was probably being held captive inside an abandoned building at one of southwest Dade's migrant farm camps. It really didn't matter where she was, though. She was going nowhere.

With her wrists shackled heavily to an overhead pipe and her legs spread wide apart with each ankle chained to a cement block, her forced captivity was worse than that of a wild animal at *Metrozoo*. The areas surrounding her wrists were reddened with welts. If the shackles weren't loosened soon, blood was sure to spill—Maureen's wrists were that raw.

Surprisingly, Maureen was dry-eyed. She had spent herself of tears at some point during the night when a cockroach had crawled down one of her raised arms, gone up her shoulder and onto her face. Not having been able to rid herself of the disease-carrying insect, she had cried herself into a standing sleep.

The front door opened. Footsteps were heard coming from the other room. Then a man appeared in the doorway. It was the same man who had kidnapped Maureen. The same Latin man who had brought her to this place of torture. It was Gustavo.

"How Rob's girlfriend is?" he asked Maureen.

She didn't give him an answer. She was too frightened to speak.

"Oh, this no goods. Rob's girlfriend must talks. I has many questions for hers." He walked towards Maureen and pulled out his MAC-10. He waved the automatic pistol in front of her face. "Now you talks."

"Why are you doing this to me?" Maureen whimpered. "Who are you?"

"I is Gustavo. I is Rob's friend."

"Rob doesn't know any Gustavo."

"Rob no tells you about me? He no says nothings about Gustavo? I no believes you." Gustavo replaced the gun in his waistband and looked nastily at Maureen. "You knows where is Rob going?"

"I don't know what you're talking about. He's not going anywhere."

"You no needs to lies to me. You jest needs to tells me where is he going."

"I already told you. I don't know anything about Rob leaving. What's going on here?"

"Mierda!" Using both his hands, Gustavo grabbed Maureen's sheer blouse and ripped the delicate fabric to shreds, exposing a lacy, rose-colored bra protecting her full breasts. "Oooh, Gustavo likes!" He pulled a chair up in front of Maureen and climbed up onto it. His hips were equal height with her chin. Unzipping his pants, he said, "If you no wants to talks, maybe you wants to sucks." Gustavo reached into his pants and pulled himself out. He waved his flesh in front of Maureen's face like he had with his gun. "Now you sucks!" he ordered.

But Maureen refused to give in. Holding herself

emotionally together, she gathered all the inner strength she could find and spit on Gustavo's hardness. She got a brutal slap on the left side of her face in return. Her cheek immediately showed signs of a purplish-black welt forming.

Gustavo jumped down from the chair and threw the wobbly piece of furniture against the far wall. He seemed to be insane, cursing and swearing in Spanish, dashing about the room in a frenzied madness.

After wiping himself of Maureen's saliva, he pushed his now-soft member back into his pants and zipped up. He then moved toward Maureen and pressed his body against hers, flattening her breasts against her chest. Backing away a few inches, he reached up with his hands and tore off her bra, carelessly tossing the ripped article of lingerie off to one side.

Again Gustavo withdrew his MAC-10 pistol and flashed it back and forth in front of Maureen. "You no tells me where is Rob going and you no sucks, so now I has to kills him. But first I fucks Rob's girlfriend with gun." Gustavo pulled down Maureen's skirt and ripped off her panties. Slowly, he brought the deadly steel barrel of his MAC-10 between her legs.

Maureen couldn't take anymore. Screaming at the top of her lungs, she tried calling for...

...Rob awoke from his nightmare on the telephone's fourth ring. His body was dripping with cold sweat as he crawled out of bed and onto the floor, fumbling around for the phone. His eyes were still encrusted with sleep. "Who is it?" he barked angrily into the receiver.

"Is me."

"Damn you, Gustavo!" Rob cursed, venting his frustration from the strangest dream he had ever had. It was as if he had been in the dream, hovering overhead from above the room's piping, seeing everything, hearing everything, witnessing the whole scene between Maureen and Gustavo. Rob was still shaking, but was glad the nightmare was over—glad it had only been a dream.

"Why you answers phone like this? What I do?" Gustavo wanted to know.

"Forget about it, okay? Why'd you call?"

"We flys tonight, my friend."

Rob jumped up off the floor, raging into the receiver, "No fucking way! It's only fucking Friday! The run's not until tomorrow night!" It had been a bad week for Rob ever since Maureen left him in Key West four nights ago. And now this.

"Maybe you no hears me first times, so I tells you again. We flys tonight."

The consequences of Gustavo's directive were sinking into Rob's brain at an electrifying rate. Since Wednesday, he had been carefully monitoring the weather, tracking the progress of an approaching artic cold front. He was almost certain that if they departed on Saturday night as originally planned, the frontal system would pose no threat to their return flight early Monday morning. But now, with Gustavo's news, the scenario was turning deadly. Rob tried explaining the situation to the Latin. "Listen, Gustavo...if we make that run tonight, it's gonna put us back over Florida on Sunday morning. That's right when this cold front will be passing through. I'm talking low-level scud, rain, poor visibility...possibly even some heavy fog. That's serious stuff. It's not like I'll be landing at a commercial strip with an ILS approach...where I got approach plates and shit like that. So give me a break and get Falcon to switch the run back to Saturday night. Otherwise there's a good chance the three of us will be flying to our deaths at Palm Bay...you, me and Nick." Rob paused for a breath, then questioned for confirmation, "That is our destination, isn't it? Where we're bringing the load to?"

"*Si*, Palm Bay." Gustavo had personally selected the site for this run's drop-off point. For the purpose of landing and unloading a marijuana-laden airfreighter, Palm Bay was perfect. Located just south of Melbourne on Florida's "Spacecoast", it had a flat and open area of land to the west of town that had been partially subdivided and strung out with a spiderweb-like network of streets back in the late 1960's, before the land boom went bust. Many of the roads were now half-hidden from years of uncontrolled weed growth. With the acreage being far enough away from the area's main populace, the subdivision made a very accessible landing site for a drug plane—on a clear night.

Rob sensed that Gustavo was about to hang up on him, so he did some fast thinking and threw a hard punch where it hurt. "You wanna die like your father did, Gustavo? Is that what you want? You want me to pancake us into the ground? 'Cause that's exactly what will happen if I try landing that plane in the middle of a cold front with no landing system other than the ADF." Rob knew all too well that flying a minimally equipped aircraft at low altitude in rain and fog was like kissing death's ass. Again he stressed his point, "You wanna die like your father did?"

"How you knows about hims?"

"Loose talk sucks, Gustavo." It was George who had told Rob of the fiery crash—the Convair 240 that had gone down in the midst of a thunderstorm.

"You no trys to tricks me?" Gustavo expressed with a hint of nervousness in his voice. "Is coming, this fronts?"

"Yeah. It's coming. And it'll be waiting for us over Palm Bay unless you get ahold of Falcon real quick-like."

"But is Falcon who says we flys tonight. No me."

Gustavo's nervousness had changed to fear. He was trying to defend his innocence in the matter. Although he did not want to die like his father, he also knew that Falcon's decisions were usually final.

"Well, can't you explain to him about the weather? I mean, he'd have to understand. He'd be risking millions if the plane went down in weather."

Gustavo didn't know how he was going to do it yet, but said, "I talks wis hims. Then I calls you back."

The telephone went dead in Rob's ear.

The International Bank of Commerce, situated on Brickell Avenue in the heart of Miami's financial district, had been the provider of a major economic boost to South Florida's Latin business community since its opening six years ago.

IBC's founder and president, forty-eight year old Rafael Ramairez, was sitting comfortably in a plush, suede chair behind his hand-rubbed, mahogany desk. The chair was turned away from the desk, giving Rafael a spectacular view overlooking Biscayne Bay through the plate glass window of his twelfth-story, penthouse office. Banking wasn't on Rafael's mind as he watched two powerboats race across the bay's choppy surface, wishing he was at the controls of the lead boat.

A few silent moments spent in front of the picture window was a daily ritual for Rafael. His chosen profession was taxing at times. Daydreaming away the pressures provided a much needed relief valve.

Despite the pressures, however, Rafael relished the fringe benefits of international finance. He loved the fast-paced lifestyle, the social events, the gorgeous women, the intrigue and the power. He loved the respect he received from others in his field. All in all, Rafael was satisfied with his worldly surroundings.

Not only was he satisfied, he was proud as well. Proud of where he had taken himself in the competitive world of corporate banking, having risen from meager beginnings as an assistant loan officer fresh out of college. Born in Colombia, but educated in the United States since his primary grades, Rafael held a Masters of Business Administration from Harvard Business School.

Throughout his banking career, Rafael's bosses had praised his controlled aggressiveness by rewarding him with promotion upon promotion until, one day, Rafael realized he had finally stalled in an upper management position. He wanted more. Much more.

Not one to sit idle, he had arranged his own financing and founded the International Bank of Commerce, becoming a multi-millionaire in the process. On *his own* he had made it to the top. *His own,* however, was not only in banking, for Rafael Ramairez led a double life. Outside his financial circles, he was known as Falcon. With birth ties to one of Colombia's strongest "families", Rafael had easily filled the role of drug kingpin.

The voice of Rafael's secretary came in clear over the desk-mounted intercom system. "Your nephew is here to see you, Mr. Ramairez."

Rafael flipped around in his chair and pressed the "SPEAK" button on the intercom. "I'll see him now. Send him in, please." Rafael got out of the chair and walked around to the front of the desk. He greeted his nephew and pointed him to a seat. Noticing Gustavo's shakiness, he asked, "Would you care for a drink?"

Gustavo shook his head that he didn't.

"Please excuse me, then, if I drink without you. It's almost lunchtime." Rafael spoke English with a near-authentic North American accent. He walked over to a fully-stocked liquor cabinet in the far corner of his office. Opening the door to a small icebox, he pulled out three cubes and dropped them into a Waterford tumbler. He drowned the ice with fine imported scotch, then stirred the drink with his finger. He walked back to his desk and stood beside it, looking down at Gustavo. "Why do I perceive we have a problem?"

Rafael listened for several minutes as his nephew explained in exaggeration about the cold front. When Gustavo was finished, Rafael again pressed the intercom's "SPEAK" button. "Tell Alec I need to see him in my office immediately," he instructed his secretary.

"Yes, sir."

Not more than a minute later Alec entered the office. Dressed in pinstripes, Alec evoked the image of a successful corporate attorney—and he was. Alec and Rafael went way back together. They had been roommates and best friends all throughout their college days at Harvard and, although each had gone their separate way upon graduation, they remained close friends, having kept in touch with constant phone calls and letters, following each other's career and personal doings.

Then, when Rafael ventured into the underworld of drug smuggling, he made Alec an offer. Alec had hesitated not an instant in accepting Rafael's terms, which had been laid out quite openly. And so, like Rafael, Alec became a millionaire.

Alec fit the bill perfectly—intelligent, respected, cool-headed, brilliant at corporate law. He was Rafael's most important asset—he was Falcon's right-hand man and confidant. Alec was somebody a man could trust with his life. Somebody a man could trust his secrets to. Alec's official title at IBC was Vice-President of Corporate Affairs.

After making Gustavo repeat his story, Rafael asked of Alec, "What do you think about my nephew letting one of our pilots give him orders?"

Very straight forward and business-like, Alec commented, "It seems as if Gustavo has lost his machismo."

"Exactly." Rafael sipped his scotch. "And Rob is getting cold feet...which explains why he emptied his account at IBC last week and purchased the Winnebago in Tampa. It looks as if your earlier assumption was correct, Alec. We've got a pilot who wants out. He's got the motorhome waiting for him in Long-Term Parking at Tampa International with two-hundred thousand stashed away inside of it and another hundred expected after this next run. It seems as if he has everything set up neat and tidy for leaving the organization. All he has to worry about now is getting through the flight safely. So now, with a little weather thrown into the picture, he gets frightened and convinces Gustavo that the system is worse than it really is." Rafael turned to his nephew, again looking down upon him. "Alec is right. You've lost your machismo."

Gustavo was more terrified of Falcon right now than he had ever been before. He was praying he could keep himself from soiling his underwear, knowing he was about to pay his dues for the mistake he'd made in coming to see his uncle.

Rafael continued, "You are nothing but an overpaid streetfighter, Gustavo. Maybe I should have left you to rot in Cartegena. But I didn't. Out of respect for my brother, I brought you over here, hoping you could fill his position in the organization. Now I see I was wrong. You have inherited your father's bad traits. You are the same as him."

"Maybe he no smarts like you, but he stills your

brother. How you can talks like dis about hims?"

"My brother...your father. He's dead, Gustavo. What does it matter?" Rafael walked over to the window and looked out at the bay. "As for the flight...arrangements are made. The aircraft departs tonight." Rafael then spun back around to face Gustavo one last time. "I want Rob eliminated after this flight," he said as easily as if ordering a pound of chop meat from the local butcher.

Gustavo understood. "I excused?" he asked, rising from the chair.

"You may leave." Falcon had to be harsh, even to family. He had no choice. The drug business left no room for disobedience. Rafael waited for Gustavo to leave the office, then asked of Alec, "What punishment do I bestow upon my nephew?"

"Nothing. Let it slide this time."

"You question my judgment?"

"There's been no harm done."

"You are wrong. There's been great harm done...to the organization, to my trust in Gustavo. His misdeed must be punished. I will think of something."

"You've ordered Rob's death. Isn't that enough? He's the one who put the idea in Gustavo's head."

"Maybe you are right, Alec. Maybe you are right." Rafael entered into deep thought for a moment. When he spoke up, he said to Alec, "Get our explosives expert out to Tampa. Have him rig the motorhome as insurance in case Gustavo fails me again."

For the first time in years, Rob answered the phone on the first ring. He knew it would be Gustavo.

Falcon's courier made his call very brief. "I sees you tonight. We flys south." No more was said as Gustavo hung up on Rob.

"Shit!" Rob cursed in frustration. Why was Falcon being so insistent upon leaving tonight? Why was he risking the load, the profit, the lives? Rob threw the telephone at the wall in anger, then trodded into his living room and plopped himself face-down onto the torn couch underneath the trailer's double-wide window.

Rob was depressed. Just thinking about the flight made his stomach quiver with weakness. He wished he hadn't eaten the salami sandwich for lunch while waiting for Gustavo's call. When he felt the sandwich creep upwards, he ran for the bathroom, reaching the toilet just in time to deposit his lunch.

Rob moved over to the sink and turned on the faucet. While rinsing out his foul-tasting mouth with warm water, thoughts of Maureen crossed his mind, adding to his depressed state. He had not seen her all week. He had not been to the Flight Deck Lounge all week. Rob missed Maureen. He thought about the letter he had written to her. Today was the day. Today he would go to the Post Office and mail the letter. He knew she would probably hate him for it, but it was the only way.

Suddenly, Rob realized he had tears running down the sides of his unshaven face—the first tears he had shed in eight years. What he didn't know was whether they were tears for Maureen or tears for himself.

CHAPTER NINE

Friday Evening

Sometimes nature played tricks on the human eye, creating wonderful illusions. Sunset was one of those times, especially on the ramp at airports. Maybe it was the way the low rays of sunlight filtered through the distant haze along the western horizon, casting shadows of the airplanes upon the ramp. A good sunset was able to make even the most dilapidated aircraft sparkle with reflected illumination. It was that kind of a sunset tonight at Opa Locka Airport.

Rob was there at the airport, waiting quietly for the sun to finish its descent. He had managed to pull himself together, but it had taken him a long afternoon of soul searching to find the strength to make the flight—to face the possibility of manipulating the airfreighter back onto the ground in rain and fog and then begin his life on the run.

Sitting inside his Blazer, Rob stared out at the DC-4, its dark silhouette outlined in a bath of bright fiery-orange, almost as if N253KY's edges were burning. On the front floorboard next to Rob was his black, leather flight bag. In it, he carried whatever he needed to get him through the next two days—navigational charts, flight calculator, two flashlights with fresh batteries, a seven-stick pack of spearmint gum and a box of a dozen glazed donuts. Two gallons of tap water were already aboard the aircraft, as there would not likely be running water where he was flying to.

When the sun finally slipped below the horizon, Rob drove across the ramp to one of the Fixed Base Operations on the airfield. He parked in front of the office and went inside to the service counter. It was time to order fuel. Lots of fuel. Enough fuel to fly the DC-4 down to Colombia and back. In actuality, N253KY wasn't a "true" DC-4 at all, but rather, it was a C-54 "Skymaster"—the original military version with short-range fuel tanks. Even with its wing tanks topped off, N253KY would only remain airborne for 2,000 miles at 75% power. Not enough for Rob to make it back to Florida. But that was no problem, for Falcon's airfreighter was equipped with a pair of illegal bladder tanks mounted inside the plane's cabin area.

A pretty face smiled at Rob from behind the counter. "Hi! Can I help you?" the receptionist asked cheerfully.

"Yeah. I need that DC-4 out there topped off with avgas. It's the white one with the faded blue stripe down its side. November-Two-Five-Three-Kilo-Yankee. And I'm in kind of a hurry, so if you can get the guys on it right away, I'd appreciate it."

"No problem, sir. How would you like to pay for the fuel? We take Visa, Mastercard, Multi-Service—"

"Cash," Rob pushed in, not giving the girl a chance to finish rattling off the list of acceptable "Plastic Pesos". Credit cards were no good in the drug trade. They left too many trails that were too easily traceable.

With the fuel order placed, Rob walked away from the counter and out the door.

As was common occurrence throughout the Fixed Base Operation industry, the aircraft refuelers were waiting in the line shack—a shambles of a room, well out of sight of the customers. Affixed to the walls of the shack were fold-outs from various pornographic publications, a couple of unframed aircraft photographs and a large centerfold of marijuana torn from the pages of *HIGH TIMES* magazine.

Huddled together on an old water-stained sofa inside the line shack were the three on-duty refuelers. They were slowly flipping through the colorful pages of the latest issue of *PENTHOUSE*.

"*Fucking A*! Check out them mounds," said one of the line guys as the page was turned. "I'd give anything to go down on 'em."

"You'd give anything to go down on a goat," his friend commented, laughing.

Ignoring the commentary, the third refueler got up to answer the wall-hung telephone. He lifted the receiver and listened to the receptionist rattle off a fuel load, then said, "November-Two-Five-Three-Kilo-Yankee...sure. I'm on my way." He hung up the phone and headed for the door.

The mere mention of N253KY by the third lineman had aroused the attention of the other two refuelers—even more so than the pictorials of nude women in the magazine. Their eyes were now focused on their co-worker as he made his exit. One of them called out, "Hey, man. You did him last flight. Why don't you let one of us fuel him this time?"

"Eat shit! I'm the one who took the call while you guys were drooling over them bitches. This fueling's all mine." He turned to exit the doorway, but before he did, he looked back over his shoulder at his friends and said, "Tell you what, guys...the beer's on me tonight." And out he went, knowing he was in on a good deal with the pilot of N253KY.

All the linemen knew him—the pilot of the DC-4. He was a lineman's dream. He was cool. He knew what he wanted. And he *wasn't* from the "Old School of Aviation"—one of the thousands of pilots who still insisted on downgrading aircraft refuelers by calling them "lineboys". But most of all, he tipped well for services rendered. A crisp hundred dollar bill for topping off the aircraft's bladder tanks. A half-week's pay for forty-five minutes of easy work. And tax-free.

The airplanes he flew were always different, but the service was the same. Every couple of months, he would bring in another old transport to Opa Locka Airport. A mechanic in a beat-up van would work on the plane for a week or two. Then, a couple of days after the mechanic was finished, the pilot would come out and order a complete top-off—always at night.

It was obvious to the refuelers that the pilot was in the smuggling trade, which was alright by them since they all smoked pot anyway. They all knew to keep their mouths shut—to not say anything to management or to the Feds who showed up at the airport every now and then looking for information. The linemen felt proud to partake in the illegal fuelings. It was their way of helping the marijuana shipments get across the border for street distribution. It was their duty.

Rob parked the Blazer in the grassy area behind N253KY. He grabbed his flight case off the floor of the Chevy truck and walked over to the plane, where Nick was already doing the preflight inspection. "How's our number two?" Rob asked. "Did George ever call you about it? He sure as hell didn't call me."

"George never calls nobody. The cowling looks clean, but I wouldn't bet a goddamned wooden nickel he worked on it. Check out the puddle on the ground. Fresh oil if you ask me."

Rob walked underneath the fuselage to the left side of the plane, then over by the inboard engine. He pulled out one of his flashlights and switched it on. Being careful not to slip on the ramp's greasy smudge, he knelt down, aimed the light beam at the puddle and ran a finger through it. Bringing the sample to his nose, he sniffed. "Smells fresh," Rob confirmed, thinking the same thought as Nick—that George hadn't gotten around to fixing the leak. Not wanting to believe it, though, he added, "It could just be spill-over from when George refilled the reservoir."

"Man, I doubt that seriously. I'll bet you he was out here a little while ago wiping down the cowling so we wouldn't know he weaseled out of his work again. If I was you, I'd go give him a call right now and harass the shit outta him."

"Why?" Rob shrugged. "What good would that do? We still have to make this flight tonight."

"It'd scare him up a bit for one thing. It'd get him to tell you if he fixed the engine or not."

"And if he admits he didn't...then what? We don't make the run? Sorry, Nick...but Falcon's not canceling this flight for anything or anybody. I've already tried through Gustavo."

Nick grumbled something under his breath, pretending he hadn't heard Rob. Then, continuing with the preflight, he stuck his head up into the nose wheel compartment and shined a beam of light all around. A shiny, metallic object reflected back at him from the nose gear retraction arm. Reaching up, he felt around and grabbed hold of a loose wrench.

After taking the tool off the retraction arm, Nick held it out in his palm and turned the flashlight on it. The wrench was a 12mm open-end from George's tool chest. Nick tried figuring out why George would have use for a metric-sized tool in the nose compartment of a DC-4. The aircraft was 100% American-built. There wasn't a single metric fastener anywhere on the plane.

More importantly, though, Nick wondered why George had left the wrench up there in the first place. If he hadn't found it, the eight inch piece of hardened steel could have kept the gear from retracting after takeoff—although, more likely, it would have just fallen to the ground. The only explanation Nick could think of was plain laziness.

While Nick finished up with his preflight chores, Rob paced about, wishing the fuel truck would show up. Gustavo was due anytime now and Rob preferred to have the aircraft fully serviced prior to his arrival. Rob swore to himself that he had told the girl at the service counter he was in a hurry.

When Rob finally spotted the avgas truck turning onto the north ramp, he walked over to the aluminum ladder hanging down from the aircraft's forward entry door on the right side of the fuselage, directly behind the copilot's bulkhead. He climbed the ladder, propped the door open and stepped inside the airplane.

Quite typical of most old airfreighters, the interior of N253KY had been "stripped-to-the-bone," looking somewhat like the skeleton of a pre-historic dinosaur from the inside out. There was no carpeting to deaden the hollow sound of Rob's footsteps as he made his way down the reinforced, bare-metal deck. The aircraft's seats, side walls and ceiling panels had long been torn from the plane and scrapped for junk. All that remained of the 1940's-era airfreighter were its frames, stringers, bulkheads and outer skin.

There was, of course, the twin installations of bladder tanks and a make-shift toilet towards the rear of the cabin, configured from a five gallon paint container fitted with a plywood seat-cover cut out in the shape of a large donut.

However, despite the less-than-economy class accommodations, Rob felt comfortable inside the aging transport. It was like a second home to him, having spent so many hours flying around in old radial-engined relics.

Rob's clothes fit his mood. He had on a pair of torn and faded jeans, a semi-torn gray sweatshirt and his good pair of leather Pumas—"Cocktail Sneakers" as Nick liked to call them.

Rob unlatched the emergency exit over the left wing and bent down to climb through the narrow opening. As he walked out onto the wing, he saw that the driver of the fuel truck had already backed the vehicle between the number one and number two engines.

Rob walked over to the leading edge of the wing, between the engines, and shouted down to the refueler that he wanted to top-off the bladder tanks first and then the mains and auxiliaries on each wing.

The lineman unreeled the hose, climbed up onto the back of the truck with the fuel nozzle in his hand and passed the hose across to Rob.

Rob, in turn, dragged the hose along the wing and through the open emergency exit. When he had the hose completely inside the aircraft, he again shouted down to the refueler—this time telling the guy to turn on the truck's PTO knob. Rob knew what it was like to work the line. He had done it himself in Clewiston, back when he was a teenager taking flying lessons. He knew it was a tough way to earn a living.

Rob unscrewed the caps to both bladder tanks.

Then, once the PTO was engaged, he started pumping fuel into the tanks, giving the lineman a chance to climb onto the wing from the back of the truck and then into the cabin through the emergency exit to continue the refueling operation.

The entire procedure, including the wing tanks, was completed in under forty minutes. While the lineman was filling out some paperwork, Rob approached him. He reached into his pocket and pulled out a wad of bills. "Don't have any 'C-notes' tonight," he apologized as he peeled off five twenties. "This okay with you?"

"Hey, Jackson was an okay kind-of-a-guy," the lineman joked.

"Yeah, that's what I hear, too," Rob added as he handed the lineman the hundred dollar tip.

"Thanks." The lineman stuffed the five bills into his pants pocket, then climbed into the cab of the fuel truck. Before releasing the emergency brake and driving away, he stuck his shaggy head out the window and called out, "See you next time."

But there would be no "next time" for Rob. His machinery was in gear. His escape plan had already been set in motion. The Winnebago was in Tampa all fueled, oiled and ready to roll. In less than thirty-six hours, he would be free from the constraints of Falcon's organization. Never again would Falcon force him to run a load of weed from Colombia to Florida.

When Gustavo finally arrived at the airport, he had with him a metal suitcase containing a specially engineered, air-to-ground communications center used for ultra-clear radio reception between the two landing sites and the aircraft. He also had his Nikon. What he didn't have was the two and a half million dollars of unmarked U.S. currency—the cash needed to purchase the shipment of marijuana. That suitcase was in Miami with Alec, who would be the one performing the actual money transfer sometime tomorrow afternoon after receiving word from Gustavo that the poundage and quality were up to specifications.

Gustavo walked up to Rob, who was trying to kick the wooden chocks out from under the left main landing gear. He was having a hard time of it. Because Nick had forgotten to remove the chocks during the preflight, the increased weight of the refueled airfreighter was pressing the wooden blocks tightly between the tires and asphalt.

"What we has here?" asked Gustavo. "Already problem comes?"

"No big deal. I'll just add a little extra power and taxi over them."

"Maybe you thinks before airplane has fuels. Then maybe dis no happens."

"Yeah, right." Rob walked away from the chocks and from Gustavo.

But Gustavo followed him. "How airplane is? You test-flys again?"

"No. We didn't have a chance. The flight wasn't supposed to be until tomorrow night, remember?"

"Is no my faults," Gustavo insisted.

Meanwhile, Nick, who had been monitoring the discussion from underneath the tail section, came over and said, "That weasel mechanic put the screws to us again, man."

Gustavo seemed puzzled. "What this weasel means? I no understands what is dis is."

Before Nick had a chance to respond, Rob answered the inquiry diplomatically, hoping to prevent a reoccurrence of what had happened on the ramp in

Houston. "It means, Gustavo, that we don't think George fixed the leak in number two like he was supposed to."

"No, man!" Nick burst in. "What it *really* means is that George is a fucking shit-bag. All's he did was change the fucking oil."

Amazingly, Gustavo kept his cool. No weapons were drawn—although, his MAC-10 was in its usual place. Punches were not exchanged. He offered no threatening remarks to Nick. Gustavo just looked over at the number two engine and simply said, "We flys now."

Rob and Nick followed Gustavo over to and up the aluminum ladder. Once all three men were inside the cabin, the ladder was drawn up into the plane, the door was closed and latched, and the ladder was secured in the cabin between the two bladder tanks. Gustavo had his suitcase and camera, Rob clutched his flight bag and Nick had his two packs of cigarettes. The three men settled into the DC-4's cockpit. The drug run was about to begin.

A few minutes later, all four propellers were spinning in perfect sync as the airfreighter taxied out for takeoff. Next stop—the Guajira Peninsula in Colombia.

The moon had not yet arisen as the airfreighter flew directly over Andros Island in the Bahamas. The autopilot was engaged, holding the aircraft on a steady course of $135°$ in the nighttime darkness. In approximately two hours N253KY would pass close by Great Inagua, followed by a course change to the right to take the aircraft safely through the narrow pass of airspace separating Cuba from Haiti. All in all, the journey down to the Guajira Peninsula would take the pilots about six and a half hours—a long time to remain seated in the confines of the DC-4's cramped cockpit.

So, with the autopilot doing most of the flying, Rob and Nick kept their alertness at full peak by finding diversion in the instrument panel. Every few minutes, they would scan its breadth, monitoring the readings displayed on the dials and gauges. Red shadows were cast upon their faces from the soft illumination of the instruments, creating a spaceship-like environment.

Occasionally, a tweak of one of the four throttle or prop levers was needed. Navigational mathematics and ADF radio tuning were continual chores. But for the most part, all there was to do was to sit quietly in the cockpit, smelling its musty odor and contemplating the "what ifs" that could possibly go wrong on the drug run.

Any man who wasn't at least a little scared on a drug flight was either a total fool or just plain crazy. Rob was frightened. So was Nick. Gustavo, too. But none of them outwardly showed it. The atmosphere floating around the cockpit reeked of nervous apprehension, blanketed by a false sense of calm. When conversation erupted in small spurts, it was usually about flying, but unrelated to the run.

"What ever happened on your flight last Saturday night?" Rob asked Nick.

"What're you talking about?"

"That dare you took with your friends. You know...the flight."

"Oh, yeah. Guess I never told you about that, huh?" Nick fiddled with the ADF knob, still not offering an explanation of his sightseeing flight aboard the "borrowed" C-46.

"Well...how'd it go?" Rob persisted. "You ever make it off the ground?"

With embarrassment, Nick answered, "We took off, alright. But not with me at the controls. Man, I was so fucking drunk I passed out as soon as I climbed inside that bitch. I never even made it a third of the way to the cockpit before falling flat on my face."

"You lost the bet, then...the five hundred bucks."

"Hey, man. You win some, you lose some. That's the life of a gambler." Nick pulled out an almost full pack of Marlboros from his shirt pocket and struck the pack against his leg, knocking out one of the cigarettes.

"I hope you're not thinking about smoking that thing in here." Rob fidgeted in his seat as he looked over at Nick with consternation.

"Yeah, I am. Why? Something wrong with me smoking?"

"There's fumes back there, Nick...from the bladder tanks."

"And this ain't your goddamned airplane. But if it'll make you happy, I'll get permission." Nick turned around to face Gustavo, who was sitting in the jumpseat. "Hey, man. You mind if I smoke?"

The Colombian didn't mind at all.

"I'd say that settles the argument," Nick smirked. And so, against his captain's wishes, he lit the cigarette. What was Rob going to do, he thought? Throw him out the window?

CHAPTER TEN

Early Saturday morning
 At six hours into the flight and with Gustavo's gold Rolex showing SAT in its display window, the airfreighter's low altitude run down to Colombia was nearing its end. The sky was still dark.
 "We got the coastline coming up," Nick reminded Gustavo. "You gonna open that suitcase soon or what?"
 Without responding verbally, Gustavo grabbed the aluminum radio case from behind Rob's seat and placed it on his lap, not bothering to unlatch the lock. He would do that in his own time.
 Rob looked over at Nick. "I'm taking the plane off autopilot. I want you to bring us in for the landing."
 "Sure, man."
 "Ready on the controls?"
 Nick planted both his feet on the rudder pedals and grasped the control wheel with his right hand. "Ready."
 Rob disengaged the electronic device. "I'll bring us in at Palm Bay. That way—"
 "Hey, man," Nick cut in, "You don't gotta give me no explanation for every fucking decision you make. This ain't no airline or nothing. Right, Gustavo?" Nick got no reply from the Colombian, so he asked again, "Right,

Gustavo?"

Gustavo didn't budge a muscle.

"Hey, you alive back there? I'm talking to you," Nick scolded abusively. Still nothing from Gustavo. "You got something up your butt?"

Gustavo just wasn't speaking tonight. There was too much on his mind—mainly, Falcon's order for him to kill Rob after the flight. And on his own Gustavo had also decided to murder Nick as well. Both his MAC-10 and Nikon were loaded.

"Fuck you, then!" Nick barked in anger. Tension was building between the three men, but Nick was showing the worst of it.

Rob pulled out his red-lensed flashlight and turned it on. Holding the flashlight with his teeth, he reached back into his flight bag, searching everywhere for the aerial chart of Colombia. After a minute of wasted searching, he found the chart right on top where he should've looked for it in the first place. His nerves were on edge.

After fully opening the chart, Rob found the area depicting the Guajira Peninsula, then refolded the chart neatly so that just the section he needed was exposed. He studied the chart carefully. Instructing Nick, he commanded, "Start a climb to thirty-six hundred feet." Although gaining altitude would plant the aircraft on Colombian radar screens, Rob was not worried. The right people had been paid the going rate of twenty-five thousand dollars for an illegal window into Colombian airspace.

Besides, a climb was necessary. N253KY's destination was not along the Guajira's flat coast, but rather, it was in Hato Nuevo, a town a little further south in the foothills of the Sierra Nevada de Santa Marta mountain range where the airfreighter would have to clear a 3,491 foot peak. That, however, was merely a pebble compared to the tallest mountain in the Santa Marta range, which peaked out at 18,648 feet above sea level. The Colombian terrain was brutal and unforgiving.

Initial radio contact was made when the DC-4 was somewhere over the Guajira Peninsula, flying level at 3,600 feet. Messages were exchanged in code, a time was arranged for the high-intensity lights to be turned on alongside the narrow 5,000 foot, dirt landing field carved out on the side of a hill, and the current pressure reading was given to Rob so that he could set it into the aircraft's altimeter, thereby giving him and Nick accurate altitude indications to prevent a midair collision with a mountainside. Many drug pilots had lost their lives by failing to get the local altimeter pressure. Rob was not that stupid.

Outside the aircraft the moon was hidden behind an upper layer of clouds so that the blackness of the sky prevented any clear sighting of the hilly terrain below. Occasionally Rob would spot the lights of a scattered village here or there, but that was about the only visual clue he had to report to Nick, whose attention was completely occupied inside the cockpit.

Nick was flying N253KY by instrument reference. Included in his continual scan of the panel were the airspeed indicator, altimeter, attitude indicator, gyro compass, turn and bank indicator and four columns of engine instrumentation. All systems were operating smoothly—even the number two engine. Nick was also carefully monitoring the ADF needle, which he was using to home in towards the airstrip at slightly less than three miles per minute.

A quartering headwind was pushing the aircraft to the east, causing Nick to constantly readjust the aircraft's heading to maintain a track which would bring the plane over the temporary signaling station set up at the landing site.

When Nick called out, "I've got needle swing," Rob knew that he meant station passage had occured. The first leg of the run was nearly over. Soon they would be on the ground.

"Okay, what's our heading?" Rob asked as he checked the panel clock for the exact time of passage.

"One-eight-seven," Nick responded.

"Alright. Fly outbound from the station on one-eight-seven for three minutes, make a standard tear-drop, then home back in towards the airstrip while descending. Take us down to twenty-five hundred and hold us there until I've got visual contact with the lights."

"What about the peak?" inquired Nick.

"It's behind us. We're clear from here on in. The strip's at twenty-one hundred, which'll give us four hundred feet on final. Any problem with that?"

"No problem."

"Good." Rob kept a keen eye on the panel-mounted clock. When it was coming up on three minutes, he said, "Okay, Nick. Get ready to start a tear-drop to the left...right about...now."

Nick flew the pattern, which once completed, put the aircraft on a four mile, basically straight-in approach to the clandestine airstrip. Nick applied nose down pressure to the control wheel, causing the airfreighter to slowly lose altitude as it cruised above the Colombian countryside south of Hato Nuevo.

As Nick maintained a steady rate of descent, Rob reached for the aircraft's "Operating Manual" which was on top of the glareshield. He turned on his flashlight and flipped the pages of the manual until he came to the "*APPROACH AND LANDING*" checklist.

"Carburetor air?" Rob called out.

"Cold," responded Nick.

"Tank selectors?"

"Mains on."

The list continued. "Crossfeed, auxiliary tanks?"

"Off," Nick answered.

Rob completed the approach part of the checklist with yet another three miles still to go before touchdown. In anticipation, he looked out the windshield once again, this time spotting the runway lights. "I've got visual," he called out.

Hearing those comforting words, Nick took his sight off the trusty instrument panel and lifted his head. He would fly the remainder of the approach by visual reference. "Gear down," he called out to Rob.

Rob hit the gear knob, waited for the indicator lights to illuminate and when they did, said, "Gear down and locked, three green, pressure up." Then, easing the power back on all four of the powerful radial engines, Rob slowed the aircraft down to 105 knots indicated airspeed before calling out the items on the landing portion of the checklist.

"Cowl flaps?"

"Set trail."

"Landing lights?"

"Extend and on," was the reply as Nick reached for the switch.

"Wing flaps?'"

"Set forty-five degrees."

With the dirt airstrip now only a mile and a half in front of them, Rob again reduced the airspeed, this time down to 95 knots. As the DC-4's proximity to the ground got closer, Rob began calling off the lessening altimeter readings for Nick. "Four hundred feet...three-fifty." The runway lights were now only half a mile away. The approach was smooth. No turbulence. Only a bit of a crosswind component to compensate for. Nothing too difficult. "Two hundred...one-fifty," Rob continued. Rob spread his right hand across the four throttle levers, ready to pull them back to their stops as soon as Nick started his flare. He read off the altitudes right on down to the threshold. "Forty feet...thirty...twenty...okay, start your flare-out."

Nick applied back elevator travel, which put the aircraft in a nose-high attitude as the main tires settled to the ground. He maintained back pressure throughout the roll-out until the plane had slowed down to about 60 knots, at which time he eased the nose down gently. It was a perfect night landing on a rugged, country airstrip.

The instant the nose wheel made contact with the ground, Rob took control of the aircraft by guiding it down the strip using the DC-4's small steering wheel located on the side panel by his left leg.

Simultaneously, Nick moved the landing gear emergency extension handle to its rear position, moved the propeller controls to full low pitch and opened the cowl flaps to help cool the engines.

Not much braking assistance was needed as the pilots allowed the aircraft to slow down on its own, using up the remainder of the runway's 5,000 feet. Being that there were no taxiways or ramp areas, Rob brought the DC-4 to a complete stop at the end of the strip, swung the airfreighter around with differential power and braking, then set the parking brakes and shut everything down. The aging DC-4 had made it safely to Colombia.

Gustavo immediately unfastened his seatbelt. Without saying a word to either of the pilots, he left the cockpit. Hurriedly throwing open the side door, he set the ladder in place, climbed down and got into a van, which had been waiting for him at the base of the ladder. Gustavo and the mystery driver then sped away down an unlit gravel road.

Rob and Nick never questioned Gustavo about his whereabouts while on the ground in Colombia. It was none of their business to know and they both preferred it that way. So, on each flight, when Gustavo left them, they remained with the aircraft, waiting impatiently for the illegal cargo to arrive. Sometimes it was several hours before Gustavo would return.

All the while, Rob and Nick would be well aware of the dozen or more armed men guarding the airfield—guarding them. It was all part of Falcon's paid protection plan, bought from the Colombian officials for using the airstrip. An insurance policy of sorts.

CHAPTER ELEVEN

Saturday morning

Sunrise was still two hours away when Rob finally exited the airfreighter. He joined Nick, who had gone down the ladder half an hour ago and was sitting on the damp ground with his back resting up against one of the main tires. Rob plopped himself onto the ground also and leaned against the opposite side of the tire. The only sounds in the calm morning air were those of a couple of guards laughing in the distance.

"One of the better strips Gustavo's picked out, wouldn't you say?" Rob commented.

"Yeah, man, 'cept for them trees down there at the other end. We're gonna be departing right for them. Better pray God's on our side for this one."

"We've got five thousand feet, Nick."

"Yeah, man." Nick closed his eyes. He was too exhausted for any more small talk—too old to be flying thirty-odd hour missions down to South America and back. To ease the effects of his tiredness, Nick drew out a cigarette and jammed the Marlboro between his lips. As he smoked the cigarette, he let the ashes fall onto his lap, not bothering to flick them elsewhere. The chain-smoking copilot had already finished off his first pack of

Marlboros since flying over Andros Island and was well into killing off the second pack.

Although reality said otherwise, all seemed peaceful at the airfield. The illusion had placed a hypnotic trance over Nick, for he was feeling tired enough to fall asleep, almost as if on a narcotic fantasy. He let out a wide yawn while crushing the butt of his cigarette into the dirt. He was looking forward to taking a long nap inside the quiet cabin of the airfreighter.

He was just about ready to get up and go into the plane when, suddenly, Rob startled him out of his near-sleep condition. The question was a strange one, Nick thought. Totally out of the blue, he mused. Nick swung himself around the tire to face Rob. "Ask me that again. I just wanna be sure I'm hearing you right."

"Have you ever thought about suicide?" A blank expression was covering Rob's handsome features. He looked autistic.

Realizing his hearing was fine, Nick put forth, "You're joking, right?"

But Rob wasn't joking. "Haven't you ever wanted to just pack it all in? Hasn't there ever been a time when you felt that life just wasn't worth living?"

"Hell, no!"

"Well, I have...a lot."

"Man, if that's how you wanna go...fine. But it ain't very poetic. Take me, for example. When I go, I wanna go either flying or fucking. And it don't matter much which one neither.

Nick's answer was not what Rob had wanted to hear. What Rob wanted was for Nick to listen to his problems and convince him that things weren't as bad as they seemed. But figuring he was asking for a miracle from Nick, Rob gave up before even trying.

Nick, meanwhile, fully expecting Rob to carry on

with his suicidal talk, and not wanting to hear it, decided it was time to make himself scarce. Standing up, he crudely remarked, "I gotta go empty my worm." Then, holding his crotch tightly with both hands, Nick walked forward, stopping when he came to the nose gear, where he pulled down his zipper, whipped himself out and pissed indifferently onto the airfreighter's nose tire. "Ah, Relief!" he exclaimed to nobody in particular, but feeling it appropriate for the moment.

After shaking off the last few drops, Nick turned back to Rob and said, "I'll be up inside this beast if you need me. I'm gonna try and catch me some *z's*." Stretching both arms skyward while yawning, Nick aimed his tired carcass towards the ladder. In a matter of seconds he was out of sight.

After not more than five minutes alone on the ground, Rob decided that sleep sounded good to him, too. He climbed into the plane, where Nick was already snoring like a walrus on the floor of the cavernous DC-4. Rob layed himself down, ready to fall asleep, but couldn't.

Instead, his mind raced with incredible speed, thinking back on the irony of his flying career and comparing it to the path he'd once imagined his profession would take. Like most young pilots, the major leagues had been Rob's goal—Delta, Eastern, Pan American, Northwest Orient and the rest. But form-letter rejection notes were the closest he'd ever come to being hired by one of the major commercial carriers. He hadn't even been called out for a single interview.

Instead of piloting modern jetliners to romantic places like Paris, Honolulu and Hong Kong, he'd spent years flying pistons to back-hole Latin destinations like Managua, San Salvador, Barranquilla and dozens more, with most overnight layovers usually spent in roach-infested motels. Funny thing, Rob thought, was that even those sleazy motels were like Hiltons compared to where he was trying to fall asleep now—on the dirty cabin flooring of a tramp airfreighter.

As if chilled, but knowing he wasn't, Rob felt a terrible shudder flash through his body. At first he thought it was caused by what he had been thinking about. But the more he picked his brain, the more he realized the shudder had been brought on by something else. Something more substantial. He shut his eyes and reached far into his subconscious, pulling out hidden thoughts and placing them into the realm of consciousness. Then it came to him. His private inner thoughts were of armed guards—the ones outside the aircraft. Rob figured those were the thoughts which had caused his sudden shudder, although he wasn't certain. Whatever it was, Rob was ever so glad that this was his last flight for Falcon.

He then switched his thoughts momentarily to his escape plan—to how he was going to use his drug money as a magic carpet to freedom. He had all his cash stashed away inside the Winnebago, all in hundred dollar denominations with non-consecutive serial numbers. Each bill was going to be another thread of the carpet in which to buy his survival while on the run. He pondered how long the carpet would last before the last thread was pulled. He wondered, too, where he was going to settle—if he was going to settle. And if he would ever fly again.

Flying, after all, had been such a major part of his adult life. Never having gone to college or trade school, it was the only job skill he knew. On the other hand, flying was what had gotten him into this mess in the first place. Maybe it was time for him to learn a new trade. Perhaps he could be a fishing guide somewhere.

Deep down, though, no matter how much he'd been disillusioned by the politics of airline hiring, Rob knew he would miss flying if he was to give it up. To him, there was nothing quite like manipulating the controls of an aircraft. Even his first airplane ride was still very much alive in his memory—more so than his first fuck was.

Robbie had been a young boy of eleven years whose parents had resettled in the farming town of Clewiston, bordering on the southwestern edge of Lake Okeechobee in South Florida. Not knowing anyone in his new neighborhood, Robbie had jumped on his bicycle and gone exploring down the narrow Hendry County backroads, where he stumbled upon the town's tiny airport.

It was there at the airport that the proud owner of an immaculately restored Aeronca C-3 "*Flying Bathtub*" offered to take Robbie on a short flight around the patch in his two-seater, high-winged airplane. Once in the air, however, upon seeing the excitement sketched on the boy's face, the old-timer decided to extend the flight. And so, together—man and boy—they performed dutch rolls, 360^0 turns, stalls and finally, after gaining some altitude, a gentle power-off gliding spiral down to five hundred feet.

When power was again added and the antique aircraft leveled off, the old-timer took Robbie on an aerial tour of nearby towns. Northwest to Moore Haven and Arcadia, south to Immokalee, then a swing to the northeast for a landing back at Clewiston. The flight was a perfect triangle—a triangle which Robbie knew he would never forget. He decided right then and there that someday he, too, would be a pilot.

When the intense afternoon heat woke Rob up, he was surprised to find out that it was two o'clock. He couldn't even remember having fallen asleep, let alone having been out of it for nearly seven hours. He rubbed his eyes before fully exposing his retinas to the bright sunlight flooding him through the open cargo doors. Looking around the cabin, he saw that Nick was awake, smoking a cigarette, sitting with his back up against the rear bulkhead.

Rob felt sweat rolling down his back. His sweatshirt was soaked. He rose from the airfreighter's dirty floor and walked over to the open doors. He looked outside and, not seeing the marijuana, asked Nick, "Where's Gustavo...and the trucks?"

"Hey, how the fuck do I know? I ain't his babysitter."

"Doesn't he know the longer he holds us up here in Colombia, the more chance we have of running head-on into that damned cold front?"

"Cool down, man. It's not as big a deal as you're making it out to be. You know them Flight Service forecasters are always exaggerating everything to cover their asses."

"Maybe so, but I wanna be in the air by six o'clock to beat that system to Palm Bay."

"Yeah? And what if Gustavo ain't back by them? We just gonna say *'fuck you all'* and takeoff?"

Rob didn't answer. He sat back down. But soon, after realizing his stomach was making gurgling noises, he got back up again and walked forward to the cockpit. He opened his flight case, pulled out the box of donuts and strolled slowly back to the rear of the cabin. He sat down beside Nick. "You hungry?"

"Yeah, man. You got them glazed ones again?"

"Yeah."

"I'll take three of 'em."

Rob took two donuts for himself, then passed the box over to Nick. "Here. Take what you want." As Rob ate the two sugary rings of dough, his mind worked vigorously trying to put a finger on his depression. Finally, it came to him. Idleness. That was the problem. Depression always hit him during periods of full-blown idleness. If he could somehow manage to keep himself constantly active, then maybe—just maybe he could maintain himself in an equilibrium condition. No highs, no lows. A steady-state.

Just then, a commotion started outside the airplane and along the entire length of the airstrip. The guards had all moved into strategic locations, with at least seven of them surrounding the airfreighter. Shouting to each other in Spanish, the armed guards readied themselves to spray bullets into the sides of a dust-encrusted truck which was traveling at a high rate of speed towards the DC-4.

But there was no need to shoot. As the vehicle got closer, the guards recognized Gustavo's grinning face smiling at them from the passenger side of the truck's cab. Aboard the back of the truck, hidden beneath a cover of vegetable crates, was a valuable load of high-grade Colombian gold—a third of Falcon's shipment. The other two-thirds would arrive shortly aboard additional trucks.

The first truck was carefully backed up close to the airfreighter's cargo doors. Within seconds, several muscular men had pulled themselves onto the rear of the flatbed and were busy dumping the vegetable crates over the sides and cutting the metal straps holding down the bales of marijuana.

A second crew of strongly-built men were already inside the DC-4's cabin, ready to accept the illicit cargo. Soon, in assembly line fashion, bale after bale of marijuana was passed along from the truck to the man in the airfreighter's doorway, to another man in the cabin, and then to yet another man who was stacking the bales as far forward in the cabin as they would go.

Halfway through the loading, Rob and Nick left the steamy interior of the DC-4 and went outside into an even steamier Colombian afternoon.

"My friends. You worrys where is Gustavo was?" Gustavo had approached the two pilots from their blind side.

Nick spun around, bursting at the seams with uproarious laughter. He blurted out, "Why don't you learn to speak English like a white man, Gustavo?" He then continued on with his laughter, his overhanging beer-belly shaking in rhythmic waves beneath his sweat-soaked pilot's uniform.

"*Hifueputa!*" Gustavo shouted back, pulling out his MAC-10 and pointing it towards Nick, but not directly at him. "Don't fucks wis me!" he added. Gustavo then fired off several rounds from the automatic pistol, purposely missing the copilot's toes by inches. The shots were warning shots advising Nick that his time was coming—soon.

Surprisingly, Nick stood there smiling, taking everything in as if it were just a game. He showed no sign of fear—no indication of terror.

Rob, meantime, after having jumped back about ten yards during the shooting, couldn't get over his copilot's reaction. And what about the shooting, Rob thought? Was it an omen of things to come? Rob tried forgetting the familiar sound of Gustavo's MAC-10, but couldn't get the deafening ring out of his ears. He hoped he would never hear it again. Getting back to Florida couldn't come soon enough.

CHAPTER TWELVE

Saturday afternoon
    It had been over an hour since the last of the bales had been taken off the second delivery truck and loaded onto the airfreighter, but still there was no sign of the third vehicle. Something was wrong and Gustavo sensed it as he paced nervously back and forth beside the dripping number two engine.
    Rob sensed it, too. He gazed up at the sun for a rough time estimate—four-thirty in the afternoon—then walked over to Gustavo. "I'm starting the engines at six o'clock sharp."
    Remembering how Rob's suggestion about the cold front had gotten him into hot water with Falcon yesterday, Gustavo took badly to Rob's new command. "You no tells me nothings. I is boss. I says when is engine starts."
    Rob offered no outward resistance. Inside, however, he was planning otherwise.
    The third flatbed finally showed up with its load of marijuana at five-thirty-five. The driver was a boy of no more than fourteen years of age. Almost immediately, Gustavo laid into him with a barrage of Spanish obscenities, not bothering to hear out the boy's excuse of a

blowout.

Within seconds, though, Gustavo had forgotten about the boy. He pulled himself up inside the cabin and supervised the loading of the remainder of Falcon's shipment.

At quarter till six, Rob and Nick made their way for the DC-4's cockpit. By six o'clock, Rob was antsy in his seat. He leaned over and stuck his head out the side window, straining his neck muscles as far as he could to get a glimpse of what remained on the back of the truck. Five bales more to go. Five bales too many. Rob commanded to Nick, "I'm starting the engines." Then, for comfort, he asked, "You with me on this?"

"Go for it, man!"

For the first time in days, a hint of a smile came across Rob's face. He was glad Nick was going along with his bold maneuver. "Okay, then. Let's go for it."

Rob and Nick looked like a tight-knit, well rehearsed team behind the controls of N253KY as they ran through the checklist, readying themselves to fire up the number three engine hanging inboard on the right wing.

With the checklist completed and the magnetos switched off, Nick engaged the starter. He watched observantly out his side window as the prop swung through six blade turns, carefully checking for any signs of stoppage or hesitation, which would have been caused by oil hydraulicing in the cylinders. There was none. So, on the seventh blade swing, the mags were turned on and the boost pump was switched first to low in order to charge the fuel lines and then to high. Nick primed the number three a bit until the engine finally coughed, emitting a cloud of blue-black smoke from its exhaust system. As the majestic old radial caught on, Nick momentarily released the prime switch before again allowing the engine to run on prime.

Rob paid close attention to his copilot's actions while also keeping a sharp eye on the engine's RPM indications. When the revolutions were up to six hundred per minute, he smoothly moved the mixture control from idle cut-off to auto lean. Immediately, he checked the gauges for oil and fuel pressure. When Rob called out that he had positive readings on both dials, Nick released the starter. "Okay, there's our drop," said Rob, referring to the expected decrease in RPM. With the drop came the release of the primer switch by Nick.

Rob again scanned the oil pressure. It was indicating in the normal range, as were all the gauges for the number three engine. "Everything in the green," Rob called out. And with that, Nick advanced the throttle lever, bringing the engine up to 1,000 RPM. The entire procedure, though seemingly complex, had taken but a few seconds.

"Clear on four?" asked Rob.

Nick checked outside his window to make sure nobody was standing in the propeller's deadly path. "Ready on number four," came his reply. The starting sequence was then repeated for engine number four.

Meanwhile, back in the cabin, Gustavo was busy yelling at the loading crew as they hastily stacked the last few bales inside the heavily loaded airfreighter. Gustavo wanted them to secure the bulky cargo with nylon straps, but despite his threatening demands, the workers refused. Instead, they jumped onto the back of the empty flatbed and ordered the boyish driver to tear away from the plane before the crazy American pilots had a chance to blast them with the number one and two engines, which both still remained to be started.

Angered by the loading crew's refusal of his orders, Gustavo slammed shut and latched the huge cargo doors, then crawled up and over the bales of marijuana, making his way forward to the flight deck.

Rob and Nick had just fired up engine number one and were beginning the starting sequence for number two when Gustavo burst in on them. "Why you starts?" the Latin screamed in fury. "I tells you no to starts 'tils I says. Why you starts?" he fumed. Gustavo was standing behind the pilots, brandishing his MAC-10. "I kills you boths!" he shouted in disgust at the two rebellious flyers.

Rob and Nick ignored Gustavo's threats as the number two came to life, its gauges registering normal. From all visual and audible indications, both pilots assumed the powerplant was running smoothly. But it wasn't. During the excitement of Gustavo's shouting, Rob had failed to see the propeller's hesitation during its blade swing and had engaged the starter with oil accumulations still in the number seven cylinder—the cylinder George was supposed to have fixed.

Neither pilot had any way of knowing that they had accidentally caused a hydraulic and that the connecting rod inside the number seven cylinder was distorted. Maybe the engine would last a few minutes, maybe a few hours. The "what ifs" of drug running were starting to set in.

With the four powerplants idling steadily at 1,000 RPM, Nick turned around to rebuke Gustavo's threats. "Hey, horseshit breath. You kill us and who's gonna fly this bitch back to Florida?" Anything to provoke—that was Nick's way.

"I no kills you here, but I kills you. I swears to Jesus I kills you." Gustavo tucked the weapon away, sat down in the jumpseat and buckled himself in.

"Over my dead grandma's grave you'll kill me," Nick chided, trying to sneak in the last word.

But it didn't work as Gustavo came back with even more abusive words, then Nick, then Gustavo again.

It finally took Rob, as captain of the airfreighter, to end the verbal conflict. "Look, I've had enough *bull* outta both of you. Unless you two don't mind ending up as fertilizer for those trees down there off the other end of the runway, I'm gonna need all the concentration I can round up for this damned take-off. And even then, getting this plane off the ground is gonna be hell."

Rob wasn't joking either. N253KY was exceeding its maximum allowable take-off weight by at least a couple of tons. The DC-4's take-off from Colombia was going to be borderline at best. The airfreighter was just too damned heavy. It would have been a different situation had the plane been a DC-6, the much larger and more powerful sistership to the DC-4—but dreaming was for fools.

Once the cockpit atmosphere had settled down, Rob commanded Nick to go back into the cabin and remove the four overwing hatches. Usually used as emergency exits, Rob wanted the hatches removed during the long northerly flight to ventilate the plane of the marijuana's putrid stench.

While Nick was gone from the cockpit, Rob pulled out the aerial chart of Colombia from his flight bag. He wanted to check his departure route one last time—just to be sure. With the airfreighter's extreme heaviness, Rob knew the plane's rate-of-climb was going to be sluggish. Flying an initial northward path across the Santa Marta mountain range would be impossible. Instead, Rob planned on heading east over level ground, slowly gaining altitude before making the turn to the north. Rob put the chart away. He was satisfied with his judgment.

Nick re-entered the flight deck. He strapped himself into the right seat. "Man, it's a mess back there," he muttered.

"Yeah. Let's go home," Rob added in a hushed tone. He was ready. He was more than ready. Rob stepped firmly on the brakes as he advanced the four throttle levers to their maximum power settings. As he did, the DC-4 strained unnervingly—violently—but did not budge even a fraction of an inch under Rob's heavy braking action, although it wanted to. The aircraft wanted desperately to lunge forward, like a race horse anticipating the opening of the starting gate, but Rob would not let it.

Then, when Rob felt the time was right, he pulled his feet off the brakes. N253KY started moving down the bumpy, dirt airstrip, its speed increasing, slowly at first, then with intensified vigor.

Both pilots monitored the instrument panel, only occasionally bothering to look out through the windshield to see the distant trees looming nearer.

The airfreighter continued to barrel down the runway, eating up more and more dirt with each passing second. In the cockpit, needles wavered, dials wound up, but the airplane was still nowhere near take-off speed.

"Come on, you whore!" Nick grunted, trying to coax a few extra knots of speed out of the airfreighter. Sweat was beading up, dripping from his forehead, filling his full beard. With only a thousand feet of runway remaining, Nick's future didn't look too promising—nor did Rob's or Gustavo's.

While Nick cursed expletives at the airplane, Rob tried figuring out a way to get N253KY airborne. A normal rotation spiced up with a lot of luck was one answer, but the probabilities of success were doubtful. After much racing, sorting, deciphering inside his brain— all taking place in a matter of tenths of a second—Rob finally came up with one other way. Ground effect. It was a basic aerodynamic principal used by pelicans to skim low, just inches above the ocean's surface, while searching for a quick and easy bite to eat.

If Rob could do the same—if he could somehow pry

N253KY a few feet off the dirt strip and quickly level the aircraft in ground effect, he might just be able to save his ass. It was worth a shot. Hell, it was the only shot he had. Looking out the windshield at only four hundred feet of airstrip, Rob wasted no time explaining his actions to Nick. Swiftly, he hauled back on the control wheel, forcing the lumbering giant off the ground, hoping he could keep it there. He could, for N253KY was airborne and holding altitude.

But Rob's problems were not over yet, for the trees beyond the end of the runway were looming directly in his flight path. He dared not risk banking away into a turn, lest he stall the aircraft at such a deadly low altitude. Again, he had only one chance. With all four powerplants straining furiously at 2,700 RPM, Rob applied back pressure on the control wheel a second time. "Come on, climb. Get up there," he pleaded out loud. The DC-4 responded by gaining another ten feet of precious altitude.

But when N253KY's wings began shaking in a pre-stall buffet, Rob was forced to ease up on the wheel, causing the airfreighter to settle a few feet. A jarring strike was felt throughout the aircraft as the landing gear clipped a path among the treetops. Although a crash was expected by the crew, N253KY miraculously stayed airborne, even to the point of building enough airspeed to climb away from further danger. They were on their way home.

"Gear up," Rob called out to Nick. "Let's get this plane cleaned up and really flying."

Nick obediently flicked the gear lever, hoping to see all three indicator lights change from green to red. But Nick could hope all he wanted—the "what ifs" were taking over. "We got two reds, one green," he dutifully informed his captain. "Our left gear's hanging. Looks like them trees back there did a number on us."

"Shit!"

Assessing the situation, Nick commented, "Man, the drag from that hanging gear is gonna bite into our fuel reserves pretty good."

"Yeah," Rob agreed in resignation as he nursed the aircraft up to a hundred feet of altitude. What else could he say?

Throughout the entire takeoff ordeal, Gustavo had been speechless, but not because he'd been scared. He wasn't—no more so than usual. To him, it had been a routine departure from a drug strip—hairy. So, with the plane now in a positive rate-of-climb, he was ready to start the celebration. Opening up the metal suitcase containing the communication equipment, Gustavo pulled out the warm bottle of Dom Perignon he usually had stuffed inside. He popped the cork and guzzled a soothing mouthful of the bubbly liquid, utterly enjoying himself and feeling high with glory. His glory, for he had pulled off another run for Falcon. "You shares drinks wis me," he said to the two pilots, offering them his champagne, knowing coldly that it would be their last drink. "We drinks for Falcon."

"Hand me that Dom." Nick accepted the champagne with pleasure, swallowing enough for two people. "You want some, Rob?"

"Nah."

"Good," Nick said, laughing, "'Cause I already drank your share anyhow." He was about to take another swig from the bottle when a terrifying bang shook the aircraft, causing the champagne to spill from Nick's mouth and foam up in his beard. "Man, what the fuck was that?"

What it was was a blown engine—the number two. The strain on the engine had finally been too much for the bent rod inside the number seven cylinder, snapping the rod and shooting the piston clear through the top of the cylinder head.

Reacting cooly and instinctively to what he knew must be a blown engine, Rob scanned the instrumentation, recognized the number two as the wayward powerplant, shut it down and feathered the propeller. "Damn!" he cursed.

"Where this puts us?" questioned Gustavo, who had witnessed in-flight engine shut-downs before—some serious, others not.

"I don't know," Rob answered honestly. "The plane's still flyable, if that's what you mean. I'll have to use differential power settings to compensate for adverse yaw," which was what he was doing as he spoke. "I don't know," he said again. "I just don't know."

And the plane continued on.

CHAPTER THIRTEEN

Saturday night

Rob was looking out the windshield at fragmented land forms off the aircraft's starboard side. A three-quarter moon was shining down upon the island chain, giving Rob a clear affirmation of the airfreighter's exact position—three to five miles west of Great Exuma in the Bahamas, more than halfway home to Florida. The altimeter was registering five hundred feet. "Beautiful, aren't they?" Rob commented.

"They look the same to me," remarked Nick as he reached into his shirt pocket for his Marlboros. But the pack was empty. "Fuck, man! I thought I had some more."

"More what?"

"Cigarettes." Nick crumpled up the empty pack and threw it on the cockpit floorboard. Then, always one for an eye-opening gag, he reached down between his legs, rolled down his left sock past his ankle and unpinned his artificial foot. "Trade a foot for a cigarette," he joked, tossing the limb up and down, its shoe and sock still intact. Then, turning around towards Gustavo, he offered, "You want my foot? You can use it for target practice, 'cause that's the closest you're ever gonna come to firing a slug into me."

"You is braves, my friend. But you is wrong. I shoots you. You sees." Gustavo broke out in a smile thinking about the copilot's foolishness.

Nick wasn't fazed, though. He set the foot down in his lap and looked over at Rob. "Did I ever tell you the baby chicken story?"

"Which one? You got hundreds of chicken stories."

"The blenderizer one."

"If you did, I don't remember it."

"Man, you're gonna love this one. You too, Gustavo," Nick added after again turning around to face his Latin rival. "You're gonna appreciate the gore. It's right up your alley...and it's *all* true."

Before beginning with his tale, Nick briefly scanned the instrument panel, doing a double-take on one of the fuel flow meters because he thought he'd seen it flicker unsteadily. But when he looked back at the gauge a second time, the needle was fine. He noted in his mind to keep an eye on it.

Nick began, "I used to have this job flying baby chickens down to Nicaragua for some poultry farm down there in '*Banana Land*'. I'm talking *tons* of baby chickens and, man, can them little fuckers stink up a plane real fast! Anyway, one day I got this weirded out captain who tried telling me that them chickens had feelings like people did. I mean, he was really serious about the whole thing. He just drove me crazy with his talk. So, to get him straight, I decided to prove that chickens had no feelings. I grabbed the crash ax, went back into the cabin and tore open one of the waxed cardboard boxes that them birds were kept in. I pulled out two juicy fuckers and brought them back to the cockpit with me."

"Don't tell me...you chopped off their heads with the

ax." Rob was accustomed to Nick's gross ways.

"Hell, no! I slid open the side window and tossed them right into the spinning prop blades. Blenderized them fuckers all to hell. Man, you should've seen it. And then you know what? That captain wasn't even convinced that them chickens didn't feel anything. They couldn't have. It happened too fast."

"You're sick!"

"And you're just a pussy, Rob." Nick turned around. "You like the story, Gustavo?"

"*Si,* I likes."

Nick smiled with the satisfaction that at least somebody enjoyed his humor. "You know something, Gustavo?" Nick remarked emphatically. "You and me could probably be friends if we didn't hate each other so much."

Gustavo ignored Nick's insight.

A quiet hush filled the cockpit until Rob said, "Nick."

"What?"

"Put your foot back on."

Nick's gag had worn itself thin. He reattached the limb, making sure to lock it in place with its stainless steel pin. Then, once more, he scanned the panel. Suddenly, Nick bolted upright in his seat, pointing towards the central panel area. "Hey, did you see that?" he asked Rob.

"See what?" Rob was checking where Nick's finger was pointing, but all the gauges were reading normal— except, of course, for the column of dead instruments belonging to the number two engine.

"Man, I swear I saw the fuel flow for number four jumping around. It happened a couple of minutes ago, also. Didn't you see it?"

"No."

"Maybe it's just a faulty gauge then."

"Maybe. It's reading alright now. Let's just monitor it closely for awhile and see what happens." Rob thought that perhaps Nick's mind was playing games with him from over-exhaustion. Fatigue was deadly in the flying business and they were both in extreme need of rest. It was almost Sunday morning and they had departed Opa Locka Airport on Friday night. On the other hand, maybe Nick *had* seen the gauge fluctuate.

Not sixty seconds had elapsed when Rob shouted out, "We've lost fuel pressure on number four." At the same instant, the red fire warning light illuminated. The fire warning horn, however, did not come on—another inoperative item on the aging transport.

"Number four's burning bad," Nick confirmed as he gazed out his side window, where he could see orange flames shooting furiously from underneath the cowling of the outboard engine.

Rob immediately went through the engine shutdown procedures, turned the fuel selector valve to OFF, closed the cowl flaps and hit the red feathering button on the overhead panel. But the "what ifs" of drug running won out again when the prop refused to feather. Instead, it just windmilled freely, creating much unwanted drag—and along with the drag, a critical loss of airspeed. The airworthiness of N253KY was becoming marginal.

"Arm and release the fire bottle," Rob ordered to Nick with authority etched in his voice as he pushed the throttles of the two remaining good engines to their maximum limits.

Nick armed the engine selector valve, then reached out and pulled the fire handle, causing carbon dioxide to flood the engine compartment of the flaming number four. He looked out the window. "She's still burning."

"Arm and pull the second bottle." Redundancy was a necessity on aircraft. Lives depended on it.

Nick again released carbon dioxide onto the engine. This time, his effort was successful in putting out the flames. "Fire's out," he informed Rob.

Rather than acknowledge his copilot's remark, Rob commented, "We're not gonna make it to Florida." The airfreighter was losing altitude rapidly. Everything was aiming against its staying airborne. N253KY was already down to three hundred and a half from five. "I'm setting us down on one of those islands over there," Rob announced as he banked the aircraft onto an easterly heading, pointing the nose towards the Exuma chain straight ahead. "Prepare to ditch in case I don't reach land."

"You sure we can't go on?" Nick questioned.

"You tell me how," Rob answered sarcastically.

Nick realized Rob was probably right. Without saying a word, he tightened up on his shoulder harness, readying his body for what he knew was going to be a brutalizing shock upon impact. He'd been through it before—down in Brazil.

Without warning, Gustavo commanded, "You no ditches aircraft. You takes us to Palm Bay."

But Rob ignored Gustavo's intentions. Turning to Nick, he said, "Take over the controls for a second."

Nick placed his feet firmly on the rudder pedals and took hold of the yoke, freeing Rob's hands.

After securing his harness and lap belt, Rob informed Nick, "Okay, I've got the controls again."

Nick released his inputs.

Again, Gustavo ordered, "You flys to Palm Bay!"

"Shut the fuck up," Rob rebutted sternly. "We're going down."

As the descending airfreighter approached the island group, Rob searched as far as the moonlight would allow, hunting for the best possible landing site, wishing he had more time to choose. It was hard to be decisive, but he knew he had to make a decision quickly. N253KY's altitude was running out.

Nick, meantime, had opened the dump valves and was jettisoning fuel from the wings at an incredible rate, lessening the aircraft's landing weight and lessening the chance of an intense post-crash fire. The less fuel onboard, the better their chances of survival.

With N253KY slipping below one hundred and fifty feet, Rob knew he had run out of time. He had to make a decision *now*. "Okay, I'm putting us down on that beach up ahead, about two o'clock off our nose." Although he was tense, he showed no emotional signs of fear. "Here we go. Hold tight."

Rob made a few last minute trim adjustments, then eased the power back and scanned the instrument panel one final time before focusing all his attention outside the windshield, all the while guiding the aircraft along its descent path toward the beach. He'd always heard that a crash was relayed from the eyes to the brain in slow motion, but he found that not to be true. The ground was coming up much faster than expected.

The first indication of ground contact came when the left main gear struck the sandy shore, shearing off the tire and wheel assembly and collapsing the strut. Next came a rapid settling of the left wing, its tip gouging a deep trench through the powdery, white sand. The wingtip's digging action caused the plane to swerve sideways, tearing away control of the aircraft from Rob.

Inside the cockpit, the scene was violent as all three men were tossed about in their seats. Blood spilled loosely, randomly, in quantities. No man was immune. No man was spared.

N253KY's forward momentum was considerably diminished as its tail section swung around, knocking down trees in its path. But it was a large rock outcropping that finally terminated the airfreighter's wild ride, with the copilot's side of the cockpit taking most of the impact as it smashed horrendously against the jagged formation. The stop was sudden, the G-forces strong. Luckily, the DC-4 did not erupt into a fatal fireball.

With his mind wandering aimlessly, Rob sat motionless, unable to free himself from the nightmare. Not having the strength to even open his eyes, he could see nothing of the cockpit, but was totally aware of his body's great pain. He listened for signs of life—from Nick, from Gustavo. He listened for movement. He heard nothing. The cockpit rang a deadly silence. Was it that he was the only survivor of the crash? Had Nick and Gustavo both lost their lives? Or had they made it out of the aircraft alive, leaving him for dead?

For the first time in his life, Rob wished he had never been offered the airplane ride in the Aeronca C-3. He wished he had never learned to fly. And with those thoughts running rampant through his brain, everything went black as his consciousness left him, his mind and body entering into a dark and heavy slumber.

CHAPTER FOURTEEN

Sunday morning

Rafael Ramairez paced nervously in the study of his Spanish-Mediterranean style, Coral Gables mansion. He stopped every so often beside an exquisite wooden desk. The beautifully oiled piece of furniture had been a generous gift of friendship to him from a high-ranking officer of the Colombian Air Force. Atop the desk sat an ordinary looking telephone, certainly out of place considering the rest of the room's decor. Mounted heads of wild game and sports trophies abounded the walls and shelves of the study. Flush lighting brightened rare pieces of artwork—both painting and sculpture.

With the time approaching quarter past eight in the morning, Rafael was waiting impatiently for the phone to ring. He should have received word about the flight hours ago. "What went wrong?" he barked, clenching his fists tightly and crashing them down upon the solid desktop. "Why haven't my men called yet?"

In the room with Rafael was Alec. Also in the study, standing by the locked door, was Lucifer, Rafael's personal bodyguard. Except for when Rafael was at the bank or out entertaining the ladies, Lucifer was an almost constant companion to him.

Lucifer was a behemoth of a man, skin as black as lava stone, muscles bulging beyond natural limits, strong as a Bahamian could be. The important thing about Lucifer was that he knew when to keep his mouth shut and when to talk—which was almost never. And when he did, he spoke in the poor man's English—the common dialect of Nassau's black population.

Alec was sitting comfortably on a well-cushioned sofa with a brandy in his hand to start off the new day. "Do you suppose it was a bust? Either DEA or Customs?"

"No!" Rafael responded insistently. "Not possible. Not according to my intelligence. Everything was being drawn away from the area. That's why I moved the flight up a night. Some kind of special project they had going on."

"Maybe the local cops in Brevard County got in on the action. Small towns, you know."

"No. The ones who count have all had their palms greased with plenty of green." Rafael thought for a moment. "Something else happened. I can feel it under my skin."

"You want me to call Russ?" suggested Alec. "I'm sure he must be up by now. Getting ready to go to church, I suppose."

"He's no church man!" smirked Falcon, almost breaking out in laughter, but holding back. "Russ would be lucky if God even knew he was alive."

"Perhaps. But that's not the issue here. Do you want me to give him a call?"

Rafael did not answer. Instead, he studied the lines of an ornate, ceramic box sitting on the corner of his desk. He pulled the box closer, opened the lid and pinched some of its white, powdery contents between his thumb and forefinger. He then spread out the cocaine along the edge of the desktop. Three more times, Rafael dug into the box with his fingertips. His cocaine habit was beyond forming the drug into neat, parallel lines. To him, that was child's play.

Around Rafael's neck was a solid gold chain. Securely attached to the chain was a small gold snorting straw. Also clasped to the chain was a falcon charm, its wings spread out in flight profile, a marijuana leaf clutched in its claws. It was the same charm worn by everyone in the organization only his was gold instead of black, for he *was* Falcon.

Rafael leaned over the desk, brought the gold tube up to his nose and inserted one end far up into his right nostril. He easily inhaled half the pile of cocaine. The rest entered his bloodstream through his left nostril.

Before closing the lid on the ceramic box, Rafael offered the treasure to Alec, who gladly accepted. Before the cocaine could be dished out, though, the telephone rang. Rafael pointed for Alec to answer it.

Alec obediently picked up the receiver. "Yes...I understand. Where are you now?...Okay, I'll let him know." The receiver was placed back on its cradle.

Falcon stood by anxiously awaiting the news from the ground crew. "Well?"

"It was a no-show at Palm Bay. They're at a loss as to what happened to the plane."

"Shit!" Falcon walked around to the other side of his desk and sat down in a leather chair. "Help me analyze the situation, Alec."

"I think it's a rip-off."

"Very unlikely. Rob's too smart to fuck with me."

"What about Nick? He could have pulled it off on his own. He's broke, you know."

"Sure, he could've done it alone. But he would have had to have killed both Gustavo and Rob. He wouldn't do that."

"You don't know for sure."

Falcon looked sternly at his compatriot. "What I know is that I've built this organization by putting trust in my natural ability to judge people's characters. Believe me when I say that Nick doesn't have the guts everyone thinks he has. It's all a *put-on* by him to hide his insecurities. That's all it is."

"Then either the plane got lost due to poor navigation or it crashed. There's no other explanation."

Falcon neither accepted nor declined to believe Alec's suppositions. "Call Russ," he ordered. "See what you can get out of him. It's about time he starts earning his pay."

Russell Dickinson, a special agent for the Drug Enforcement Agency, was leaning back in his chair, throwing paper wads into a waste basket in the corner of the office. The room where he sat, located inside a rented Miami warehouse, was one of several field offices used by the DEA in which to piece together the war on drugs—an impossible mission, especially in Florida where the influx of illegal narcotics was still the area's major industry. Bigger than real estate. Bigger than citrus. Bigger than tourism in dollar sales. For the men of the DEA, Sunday was as good a day to work as any, bearing in mind the impossibility of their job. Assignments were never lacking.

Up until a few months ago, Russ Dickinson had lived a straight and narrow life, maintaining an unblemished record with the DEA, always receiving excellent reviews throughout his seven year career with the agency. Numerous awards had been issued in his name for outstanding achievements in the field of drug enforcement.

Recently, however, due to personal and financial problems, Russ had pulled himself onto a dangerous highway known as the fast lane—the drug lane. He still worked for the DEA, but his loyalty was to Falcon. The large cash payments had been too enticing, too easy. Like all the others, he'd been lured into Falcon's nest because of greed.

Sitting behind his desk, wadding up another yellow piece of legal-sized paper, Russ was thinking about nothing more than the office's drab stucco walls, its cold concrete flooring and the dozen overhead flourescent lightbulbs, two of which were flickering annoyingly. Then the phone rang on his desk. "Agent Dickinson," Russ answered. Then, hoping the other agents in the room wouldn't hear him, he whispered harshly, "What the hell's going on? I thought our agreement clearly stated that I was never to be called here at the office...no matter how urgent." When Alec responded with a reason, Russ argued, "I don't care that you couldn't reach me at home. I'm not free to talk here. Give me twenty minutes and call me back. I'll be in a booth." He gave Alec the number.

"We have problems, Russ," Alec began. "Falcon's shipment never arrived this morning at Palm Bay. Any talk floating around the office about a DC-4 crashing?"

"Haven't heard a thing," answered Russ from the LeJeune Road pay phone.

"What about a bust?"

"Just minor stuff. Nothing of Falcon's caliber. Street arrests."

"Well, keep your ears open."

"Yeah, I'll also check the computers when I get back to the office. I'll give you a buzz on the beeper if I dig up anything promising."

"You do that. Falcon's counting on it." Alec then moved in with a subtle threat over the phone. "I shouldn't have to say this to you, Russ, but Falcon feels the organization's not getting its money's worth out of you. He seems to recall much grander promises when the deal was first made."

"It takes time," Russ explained. "Please express my—"

"Falcon doesn't want excuses," Alec rudely interrupted. "He has no time for bullshit. If you fuck up on this one, Russ, you're a dead man. Do you understand?"

"Yes, but—"

"No excuses, Russ."

"I understand. Tell Falcon not to worry. I'll find the plane...and the crew."

"Good." Alec paused momentarily, then said, "I'll be flying to the Bahamas this evening with Falcon. I'll be there until Tuesday. Contact me at the Nassau number the minute you hear news of the plane. Remember...there's no room for failure. Good day, Russ." Alec placed the receiver back on its cradle. He looked over at Rafael.

"You handled the conversation exceptionally well as always. Let's go to church."

CHAPTER FIFTEEN

Sunday morning

When Rob finally regained consciousness, he was shocked with fear that the hellish cockpit prison in which he was trapped appeared to be nothing more than a dark void, a world of utter blackness. His eyes wouldn't let him see. It was then that he wished he'd died in the crash, for Rob could think of no worse punishment than blindness.

He wasn't sure how long he'd been in a state of total unconsciousness, or how many hours had ticked by since the crash, or even if it was still Sunday. For all he knew, he could have been strapped to his seat inside the wreckage for days. He just didn't know. His mind was fuzzy. Probably from a concussion, he thought. He tried remembering if his head had struck the instrument panel upon impact, but he couldn't focus his attention on any one aspect of the forced downing.

Reaching up, Rob touched his forehead to make an assessment of his injuries. What he felt was a mass of congealed blood. He probed further—his ears, the back of his head, his cheeks and jaw. When he finally got around to probing his eyes, his fingers suddenly felt the substance of hope. He must have been bleeding for quite some time after the crash, because his eyelids were caked with a layer of dried, reddish-brown blood. Using his fingernails, Rob peeled away most of the heavy crust. Then, slowly, he braved cracking open his eyes.

It took him a moment to adjust his eyes to the bright rays of sunlight glaring in at him through the broken windshield, but once he realized he wasn't blind, an emotional release flushed through his body like never before. It felt good experiencing such emotion. He wondered how many years it had been since he'd felt anything even close to resembling what he was feeling now.

Although Rob wasn't blind, he wasn't without injury. After settling down from the initial on-rush of emotion, he went back to assessing the wounds to his body. He had an excrutiating pain pounding between the fingers and wrist of his right hand, which meant he probably had several broken bones to contend with—and he was right-handed.

Rob knew that if he couldn't become ambidextrious real fast, if he couldn't get his left hand to work for him in ways that it never had before, then he was going to have serious problems escaping from the cockpit's entangling bonds, for his right foot was pinned behind one of the rudder pedals. Hacking away with the crash axe seemed like his only means of gaining freedom.

His foot was jammed good. It didn't matter that his foot didn't hurt him too badly or that he didn't think it was broken. What mattered was that it was trapped in a maze of bent metal and it was up to him to free it. Before reaching across for the crash axe, which was mounted on the forward face of the bulkhead behind the copilot's seat, Rob tried desperately to relinquish the aircraft's hold upon his foot by mentally concentrating all his strength down to his right leg. He pryed, twisted, pulled and pivoted—all without success. He needed the crash axe.

Unfastening his shoulder harness and lap belt, Rob turned to reach for the axe, but instead slammed face-first into a grizzly sight. Up until now, Rob had still been operating in a partial daze and had completely forgotten about Gustavo and Nick. But now, with reality setting in, he wanted to vomit from the scene beside him. It was a living nightmare—death in the extreme.

Of the two men, Gustavo had suffered the least. Apparently, the tremendous G-forces of impact had been too much for his seatbelt, the high strain having caused its failure, throwing Gustavo out of the jumpseat and impaling him on the engine control levers. Rob choked from looking at the throttle, mixture and prop levers buried deep in the chest of Falcon's courier.

But Gustavo had gotten off easy compared to Nick's demise, for Nick had no face. Nor did he have a right side to his head, a right shoulder blade, a right arm. During the final seconds of the crash, when N253KY had smacked nearly head-on into the jagged rock formation, Nick's side of the cockpit had been stoved in and split open, ripping Nick's upper right torso into raw meat.

Emotion hit Rob once again. This time he wanted to cry—for Nick. His copilot didn't deserve to die in such an ugly way. Nick wasn't that bad of a guy. It wasn't fucking fair, Rob swore to himself. But Nick *was* dead. Another victim of Falcon's organization.

Then a thought filled Rob's head. Something Nick had said to him. You win some, you lose some—that's the life of a gambler. Nick had just lost his last gamble. *Now* it was time for Rob to win his. More than ever, Rob was determined to escape Falcon's claws. He was going to free his foot and make his way to Florida. To Tampa International Airport. To Long-Term Parking. To his waiting Winnebago. To freedom.

Reaching over Gustavo's bloodied body and across to the bulkhead behind Nick's seat, Rob tried grabbing hold of the crash axe with his broken right hand. He couldn't, though. The problem wasn't with his hand, but with his foot. With the limb caught behind the rudder pedal, the axe was six inches beyond his reach. Again, he tried. This time he fully out-stretched his body and arm until they burned with pain. Still, the axe handle was two inches beyond his fingertips. "Damn!" he cursed out loud in frustrated fury.

Rob instantly became all to aware that the burning sensation he'd felt while stretching had transferred into his veins. His blood was running on high with fear. Fear of Falcon. He knew that it was only a matter of time before someone spotted the wreckage and that once it was, the information was sure to get back to Falcon.

Rob wondered how much time he had left, for time was now his most critical enemy. The longer he remained trapped inside the cockpit of N253KY, the better were Falcon's chances of discovering his whereabouts. And discovery meant death for Rob.

Rob knew he had to keep calm if he was going to survive his ordeal. He had to keep his mind active, working, thinking. He had to plan ahead. Stagnancy was a nail in the coffin.

That the wreckage had not already been discovered could only mean two things to Rob. The first was that the island he'd crashed on was uninhabited. This was a very real possibility, since he knew he'd set the plane down somewhere in the Exumas, a chain of islands strung out in an almost unbroken band of cays for some ninety-odd miles. With more than three hundred tiny islands running southeast to northwest, the chain had many unsettled spits of land less than a mile in length.

The second possibility was that if it was still Sunday,

the same day as the crash, and if the island *was* inhabited by Bahamians, then the islanders probably hadn't wandered onto the wreckage because they were still in church. Rob thought this theory was less plausible than the first, but it didn't really matter.

What mattered right now was nourishment. Rob was losing strength rapidly and without food and water, he wasn't sure how long he could last before passing out from the day's intense heat. N253KY was not equipped with survival rations. Even if the plane had been stocked with such standard emergency supplies as beef jerky and chocolate cubes, Rob was certainly in no position to just stroll back into the cabin to retrieve the items. Rob thought about the box of donuts in his flight case, but then remembered that Nick had finished them off during the flight up from Colombia. His predicament was looking worse each time he assessed the situation.

Rob's throat was dry, his mouth parched. The plane's two water jugs were in the cabin by the bladder tanks—if they had survived the force of the crash. And even if they did, the jugs were of no use to Rob as long as he remained a captive to the cockpit.

Gazing through the cracked and splintered windshield, Rob thought the plexiglass would make an excellent rain catchment system. Almost religiously, he wished for rain to quench his growing thirst. If only it would rain.

Then something strange happened to Rob. Not actually to him, but in his mind. Thoughts bounced in his head from every which way. Out-of-place thoughts. Thoughts of Maureen. He had visions of her dancing beneath a cloud of stars, barefoot, wearing nothing but a white satiny dress. Or was it a gown? And why was she so happy? What accounted for her radiant glow? What did the birds mean? Maureen was holding one in each of her palms as she danced about. They were white birds. Beautiful birds. Doves.

Rob was confused, disturbed. Was he becoming delirious? The visions made no sense to him. Why would his mind even bring Maureen into play at such a grave time? After all, here he was looking down upon death's door.

Then Rob recalled the letter he'd sent to Maureen. His confusion grew even more. What day was it? Was it Monday? Had Maureen received his letter yet? Or was it still Sunday? If it was Sunday, then she wouldn't be getting the letter until tomorrow's mail. What day was it? Rob had to know.

The Rolex, Rob thought! Gustavo's diamond-studded watch was the type that had the day-of-the-month displayed across its face. Over-reacting with excitement, Rob tilted his head sideways and downward, cringing with pain, but not caring, for there shining up at him from Gustavo's left wrist was the precision-made gold Rolex. Forgetting his own advice about remaining calm, Rob hurriedly tore the watch off Gustavo's wrist, failing to notice the faint pulse beating within Gustavo's veins. The Latin gunman was not dead.

Rob looked at the watch. "Fuck!" he cursed. The Rolex had been smashed on impact. When was luck going to turn in his favor?

It had been at least three hours since Rob had first regained consciousness, but still he was captive to the tramp airfreighter. To make matters worse, he was fresh out of ideas on how to free his foot. Time was wasting away.

Rob's mind had grown too weak to be of any use to him. Full of despair and pity, he was withdrawing, pulling away from the real world and drifting into a waking dream-state, a private place in which to die. He had already convinced himself that death was imminent—his punishment for taking part in Falcon's smuggling operation.

What Rob couldn't understand was why the thought of dying sounded so peaceful to him? Had his life really been so terrible that death would be a relief? Or was he just tired of life's ups and downs, with mostly downs in his case?

A sharp noise startled Rob out of his tranquility. Then, when he heard the noise again, he was able to pinpoint it to the left side of the aircraft. The sound definitely had a metallic ring to it, as if something was hitting up against the outer skin of the fuselage.

Turning to look out the side window, Rob had to squint his eyes almost completely closed to compensate for the midday sun's bright reflection off the white sandy beach. The image he saw caused him to swear he was hallucinating. Out beyond the glare of the sunshine, standing between the curled propeller blades of the number one and number two engines, was a young white girl clad only in a bikini—a very brief bikini. By the innocence of her face, Rob guessed she couldn't be more than fifteen years old.

Thinking that his mind was playing tricks on him, Rob rubbed his eyes until they hurt, then looked out again, expecting the vision of the girl to be gone. But she wasn't. She was still out there standing between the engines. This time, though, the teenage girl was also glancing up at him and her mouth was moving. Rob could barely hear what she was saying through the cracked windshield, so he slid open the side window.

"—any help...'cause I've been throwing shells at the side of your plane for five minutes and I guess you couldn't hear me. Are you hurt real bad?"

Although Rob knew the girl was anxiously awaiting an answer, he couldn't give her one just yet. Having mentally prepared himself for death, he needed first to alter his present state of being. Escape was possible with the girl's help, but only if he could reverse his cycle of thought. He closed his eyes.

When Rob was ready, he again looked out at the girl. "What's your name?" he asked politely.

"Susan Baker." She walked up closer to the cockpit. "Are you hurt? My father's a doctor. I can get him if you want. Our sailboat's anchored in the bay on the other side of the island, just over that hill." She was pointing to the hill. "Do you want me to get daddy?"

Medical attention sounded good to Rob, but first he had to find out a few things about the girl—*and* her father. After all, the aircraft wasn't exactly carrying an everyday load of cargo. Testing Susan, he questioned, "Are you cool?"

At sixteen, Susan Baker was anything but naive when it came to street talk. She understood exactly what Rob meant. "Yeah, I party. Why?"

"What'd you do?"

"Grass, coke, 'ludes." She'd even done a few hits of acid recently, but had had bad trips on it, so she didn't mention the LSD to Rob. Again, she asked, "Why? How come you wanna know all this?"

"'Cause my right foot's stuck and I need your help to free it and I don't want you freaking out on me when you see what's inside the plane."

"You a doper?"

"I was," Rob admitted in the past tense. "This was my last flight."

"Radical!" Susan exclaimed, feeling as though she'd just struck the mother lode. She hadn't smoked a joint since the first morning of the cruise—the morning her father had dumped her stash of weed into the ocean outside of Bimini. And now, here was a whole plane load of marijuana. "Where's the stuff from?" she asked inquizzically.

"Colombia."

"North or south?" Susan questioned further.

"North." Rob was bewildered by Susan's knowledge of the drug trade.

Still probing, trying to narrow down the drug's origin and knowing she was getting close, she asked, "From Santa Marta or Guajira?"

"Santa Marta."

"Quality stuff," she added, looking at Rob with begging eyes.

"Don't even ask. You can't have any. I've never pushed the stuff and I'm not about to start now."

"Why? It'll be like a reward for helping you out of the plane."

"Does that mean you won't help me unless I let you take some pot?"

"No. I'll still help. But I just don't—" Susan dropped her persistence about the marijuana, thinking the guy would change his mind later. "Hey, I don't even know your name. You asked me mine but never told me yours."

"Rob."

"Rob. That's a nice name. Rob." She smiled, then asked, "Rob what?"

"Jensen."

"Rob Jensen. Yeah, that sounds better than just plain Rob."

"What if it was just plain Rob?"

"Then I'd still like your name because you're a doper and you probably have a gun and if I told you I didn't like your name, you'd shoot me. Right?"

"Wrong. This isn't the movies."

"Oh," Susan sighed, almost sounding disappointed that Rob didn't fit her image of a doper—a New Wave cowboy with automatic firepower always at the ready. "Then there's no gun in there?"

"I didn't say that. I just said I didn't have one."

"Then there *is* a gun in there?"

"Yeah. Somewhere."

"What kind?"

"Why? Do you know about guns like you know about the drug trade?"

"A little. I've been around."

"Then it's a MAC-10."

"No doubt!"

"You just gonna stand there looking amazed or are you gonna come up here and help me get my foot loose?" Rob was starting to become impatient with Susan's questioning.

"I'll help. What should I do?"

"Go to the back of the plane. There's two cargo doors there. Turn the handle on the forward door up and counter-clockwise. The door should open."

"Okay."

Rob watched as Susan walked out past the wingtip and over toward the back of the plane, disappearing from his sight. He wondered if her father—the doctor—would be as enthusiastic and understanding as she was? Probably not, Rob thought. At least not if he found out about the cargo.

After several minutes, Rob saw Susan rounding the wingtip with a frustrated look on her face. "What happened?" Rob called out to her.

"It wouldn't move." She walked up to the nose of the plane and looked into the cockpit at Rob. "What should I do now?"

"What wouldn't move? The door or the handle?"

"The handle."

"Which way did you turn it? Clockwise or counter-clockwise?"

"Counter-clockwise...like you told me. I'm not stupid."

"I'm sorry. I didn't mean that. Did you try forcing it?"

"Yeah. Real hard. And I'm pretty strong for my weight. I workout on daddy's Nautilus equipment three times a week."

"Shit!"

"Hey, I tried."

"I'm not cussing at you. I'm cussing at my luck."

"Oh." Susan looked around, then asked, "So what do you want me to do now?"

"Go get your father," Rob responded nonchalantly, not believing he'd said it.

"I don't think you want me to do that."

"Why not? You told me he was a doctor."

"Daddy will turn you in. When I told you about him before, I didn't know you were a doper."

"What other choice do I have?"

"Anything but getting daddy."

"Then you're gonna have to try harder on the handle."

"Why can't I just try crawling in through one of those holes?"

"What holes?"

"The two holes in the side of your plane above the wing."

Of course, Rob thought! How could he have been so forgetful? Nick had removed the overwing emergency exits while the airfreighter was on the ground in Colombia and hadn't replaced them. "Why didn't you say something about those exits before?"

"'Cause I was doing what you told me to do and you told me to open the doors."

"Yeah, but—" Rob cut himself short and laughed, even though it hurt his ribcage. Smiling, he said, "Climb up on the wing and get your little tush in here."

Susan did just that. She walked out far enough to where she could hop onto the outer portion of the wing, which was buried in the sand, then walked the length of the wing to where it met the fuselage. After managing her way through one of the openings, she stood in silence inside the aircraft's cabin, taking in the aroma put out by the tons of marijuana. She'd never seen so much weed in her entire life. Bales were scattered everywhere in a wild array, many of them split open from the crash.

"You gonna stand there all day?" Rob called back to her.

"I'm coming." Susan started towards the cockpit, crawling up and over the damaged bales. When she finally reached the cockpit and caught sight of Nick, it took all of her courage to keep from gagging. Her stomach quivered momentarily, but she was able to keep everything down.

Trying to calm Susan's uneasiness, Rob commented, "Nick was an okay guy."

"He got it pretty good, huh?"

"Yeah."

Then, pointing to Gustavo, Susan asked, "Who's he?"

"He's the 'bad guy'."

"The one with the MAC-10?"

"Yeah. It's around here somewhere."

Susan looked around for the MAC-10 but didn't spot it.

Wanting to get down to business, Rob asked Susan,

"You wanna reach for that crash axe over there? See it over there, right behind Nick's seat?"

Leaning over the jumpseat, Susan undid the leather holding straps and retrieved the axe for Rob, handing him the sharpened tool. "What're you gonna do with it?"

"Chop off my foot," he joked, releasing internal tension. Then, holding the axe firmly in his left hand, he bent forward and slowly began hacking a path to freedom. When he felt a cramp setting in, he ignored the painful warning sign and instead, continued on with his task, forgetting all else but escape—escape from Falcon. That was his big mistake.

When the contorted and overworked muscles in his left hand finally reached their limit, messages were relayed from his brain, causing the hand to give out. The axe slipped, its razor edge slicing easily into Rob's flesh just above his ankle. Blood flowed freely.

"Fuck!" Rob screamed, as he doubled over, grabbing his leg, applying as much pressure as he could to slow the blood loss. It was difficult, though, with one of his hands cramped and the other broken.

Hysterically, Susan cried out, "What happened? What happened? I don't know what to do."

"Fuck, Susan! Relax, okay? It's only a cut. Your screaming isn't gonna do either of us any good." Then, once he was sure Susan was again calm, Rob cooly told her, "What I need you to do is to make me a tourniquet and tie it around my leg, 'cause I don't think I can manage with my hands right now. You're gonna have to do it all by yourself."

"How?"

"What'd you mean, how? I thought you said your dad's a doctor?"

"He is."

"Well, didn't he ever give you training in first aid? He

must have."

"I wasn't ever interested," Susan answered defensively.

"Oh, that's just great, isn't it? Now I'm gonna bleed to death 'cause you weren't ever interested!"

"Stop yelling at me or I won't help you."

"I'm sorry, alright? I really am. But everything's starting to get to me." Rob checked his leg. The bleeding had slowed a bit. At least it wasn't gushing out at a life threatening rate anymore. "Look, all I wanna do is get the hell outta this fucking airplane."

"Well, I'll still help you...but only if you promise not to yell at me again."

"I promise."

"You swear?"

"Yeah, I swear."

"Okay, I believe you. So how do I make a tourniquet?" Susan was ready to begin her lesson.

"First thing you gotta do is tear off a strip of cloth about two feet long." Rob looked at Nick and Gustavo. He decided against making Susan tear the strip from their bloodied clothes. Then he looked at Susan. All she had on was a string bikini which barely covered her small breasts, public mound and butt. Rob released the hold he had on his leg and sat up, raising both his arms. "Here. Lift my sweatshirt up over my head."

Susan did as she was told.

Then, when Rob was bare-chested, he instructed Susan on how to tear the shirt to make the best possible tourniquet. "Good!" he exclaimed when she held out the finished product. "Okay, now. This next step's gonna be a little more difficult. Squeeze your way in here as far as you can and bend down over my right leg so that you can reach my ankle with both of your hands."

Again, Susan did as she was told. "I'm not hurting

you am I?" she asked caringly, her mid-section resting on Rob's thigh, her left hip pressing against his waist.

"No, not yet. But you will, so don't let it bother you if I scream. And watch your arms down there. There's a lot of sharp metal poking all around. Be careful you don't cut yourself." Rob grabbed Susan around her waist so she wouldn't slip and get hurt.

"Okay, I think I'm ready, Rob."

"Alright. Now roll up my jeans as far as you can on my right leg. You should be able to roll it up almost to my knee." He felt her doing just that. "Okay, Susan, now tie the strip of cloth tightly around my leg, about two or three inches above the cut."

"It's an open gash, Rob. Not a cut."

"That's okay. Just tie the tourniquet around my leg tightly." Rob winced from pain as Susan tied the knot, but he didn't let her know he was hurting.

"Done!" Susan said loudly. "Can you help me up from here?"

"Sure." He reached for her upper torso and guided her out of the cramped space.

"Thanks," Susan offered.

Looking down at his leg and seeing that the bleeding had ceased, Rob rebutted with, "I'm the one who owes the thanks. You did a good job down there."

"You told me what to do."

"Yeah, but you did it."

Susan blushed, then asked, "What happens now? Your foot is still stuck."

"Now I bend down and pick up the axe and start chopping where I left off—only this time, I'll be more careful." Within ten minutes, Rob had his right foot free. Finally.

Slowly, Susan helped ease Rob out of the cockpit and back to one of the overwing exits. Before leaving the cabin, Rob turned around and looked back towards the cockpit as if giving a final farewell to Nick. Then he climbed through the opening with Susan's help to steady him. Susan followed him out the exit. Together, they sat down on the sloping wing, leaning against the sun-warmed fuselage.

Susan put her arms around Rob, comforting him, holding him close. "Do you surf?" she asked.

Rob looked at her with puzzlement. "Where'd that question come from?"

"I don't know. You just look like a surfer to me. Are you?"

"Would you be disappointed if I wasn't?"

"I don't want you to lie to me, if that's what you mean."

"I'm not a surfer."

"And I'm not disappointed." She smiled and was glad when Rob smiled back. She leaned over and kissed him—a friendship-type kiss, not a seductive one. "Me and my boyfriend surf. We're thinking about going out to California after high school, then out to Hawaii to ride the big one... the Pipeline. You ever hear of the Pipeline?"

"No."

"It's radical!"

Rob listened as Susan went on to tell him about the Pipeline and about surfing in general, but soon he was overcome by physical as well as mental exhaustion. He closed his eyes. Although he was hurting, his pain was not overly unbearable. He'd experienced worse. At least he was alive and free, no longer a prisoner inside the musty cockpit.

But was he really free? When that question arose in his mind, the pain which racked his body suddenly increased with fervor. Was he really free? He thought about the anguish of the past few weeks. He thought about the constant stress he'd placed upon himself and the continual changes of his will to live or die.

Rob now knew that he *wanted* to live. He *wanted* to be free. He *wanted* to reach his thirtieth birthday. And he *wanted* Maureen. He thought about his love for her. Then he remembered about the letter. Why did he write it? Why did he mail it? What day was this? Was it Monday? Had Maureen read the letter yet?

Rob's thought process suddenly shifted gears, slamming into reverse. What of his escape? What of the Winnebago waiting for him at Tampa International Airport? What of Falcon? Very quickly, Rob realized he wasn't free. He was stuck on an island somewhere in the Exumas with no means of getting back to Florida. He needed a vehicle of escape. But what? How?

"—up, Rob!" Susan shouted, shaking him lightly. "Wake up!"

Hearing Susan's voice, Rob struggled with his mind, trying desperately to work himself out of his trance. Catching his breath, he said, "I'm alright. I just—" He didn't have the energy to explain.

"Just rest, Rob. Don't scare me like that. I didn't know what to do. You just blacked out on me."

"I'm okay now. What day is today?"

"It's Sunday," Susan told him.

Relief hit Rob like a rock. Since it was Sunday, Maureen hadn't received the letter yet. For some reason, that meant a lot to him, although he didn't know why. After all, the letter would be delivered to her tomorrow and he had no way of stopping it. Rob said to Susan, "I know we're somewhere in the Exumas, but exactly where?"

"Warderick Wells Cay. This beach is at the island's north end and our sailboat is anchored over in the harbor at the south end...between Warderick Wells and Hog

Cay." Susan then pointed towards a turquoise-colored body of water directly out from the aircraft's wing and continued with her knowledge of Warderick Wells Cay. "There's a wreck out there. A shipwreck...not a plane. We were supposed to dive it today...me and daddy. Mom doesn't dive. But there's a storm moving in so we're not gonna dive it until tomorrow. That's why daddy motored *C'DOCKED'R*...that's the name of our sailboat. That's why he motored it over to where it's anchored now...'cause it's a more protected harbor in a storm. We were at Hawksbill Cay last night."

Rob had only half-heard Susan's commentary. "Anybody live here?" he asked, trying to figure out a way off the island. He was thinking *escape*.

"No. All the islands around here are in some kind of a wildlife preserve. I forget exactly what it is, but people aren't allowed to live here...just visit. I wouldn't wanna live here anyway, though, 'cause daddy says Warderick Wells is haunted."

Rob looked at Susan disbelievingly.

"Well, daddy doesn't really think so, but that's what the local legends say. You're supposed to hear people singing when the moon's out. Then, when the singing stops you're supposed to hear voices. Do you believe in ghosts?"

"No," Rob told her coldly. All he believed in right now was that he had to get off the island and back to Florida. But how?

"Why are you mad at me?"

"I'm not mad."

"Then what are you?"

"Frustrated, tired, irritated, hungry, thirsty...all of the above."

"Oh." Susan then asked, "How come your plane crashed?"

"I don't feel like talking about it right now."
"Why not?"
"'Cause I don't. That's why not."
"Oh."

CHAPTER SIXTEEN

Sunday afternoon

    C'DOCKED'R was secured Bahamian-style using two anchors set port and starboard off the bow. The doubling up of ground tackle assured Doug that *C'DOCKED'R* would have minimal swing during the strong ebb and flood tidal currents that rushed back and forth through the islands regularly every six hours. Plenty of rode would prevent dragging during the storm.

    Doug and Maggie were busy aboard *C'DOCKED'R* preparing for the approaching cold front. Among several items that still needed to be secured was the windsurfer, which Doug was lashing to the port stanchions with nylon line. A twenty gallon jerry-jug of drinking water which had worked its way loose from the base of the mast was next on Doug's list of things to do.

    Maggie was securing the sailboat's multitude of lines—sheets, downhauls, halyards, etc., etc., etc. She stopped mid-stride and turned to her husband. "Kiss me, Doug."

    "What?" His mind was harboring on the approaching storm, not on his wife's affections.

    "I said kiss me. We haven't kissed or touched or cuddled since we left home a week ago."

"Mag." Doug seemed indifferent, but he leaned over and kissed her on the cheek anyway.

The Achilles inflatable was still in the water, its painter tied off to a starboard cleat on the sloop's aft quarter. Doug wanted to secure the inflatable to the foredeck, but he couldn't just yet because he needed it to pick up Susan from shore whenever she decided to come back from her morning walk, which had already stretched well into the afternoon. "It's not like Susan to be so late," he mentioned to Maggie in passing.

"You must have read my mind. I was thinking the same thing. Susan should've been back at least an hour ago. I'm worried. The island isn't that big. What could be keeping her?"

Doug could come up with only one logical explanation for Susan's lateness—drugs. Somehow she must have hidden some aboard *C'DOCKED'R* and taken the stuff with her to shore. But how did she manage to hide it from sight when he'd brought her to the island in the Achilles? She hadn't taken a towel with her—not even a small lunch bag. "Mag, tell me if I'm wrong, but wasn't Susan wearing her black string bikini this morning? The tiny one that doesn't leave much to the imagination?"

"Yes. Why do you ask?"

"Bare with me for a few minutes, Mag. I'm trying to figure something out."

"Well, tell me, Douglas. If it's about Susan, I have a right to know."

"Mag, I have a fairly good idea why Susan's not back yet. I'm hoping to God I'm wrong, though."

"What is it? Do you think she's injured?"

"No...not injured." Doug was stalling.

"Well?"

Doug looked over towards the lush green vegetation covering the island's gentle rolling hills. When he finally turned back to his wife, he said, "I think Susan's high on drugs."

"But..." Maggie was lost for words.

"Mag, if it's true, it's my fault." Doug then proceeded to explain about the incident which happened over a week ago outside of Great Isaac Light and Bimini, when he'd caught Susan with the baggie of joints and how Susan had promised him she had no more, and why, upon reaching Bimini, he'd decided to continue on with the cruise while keeping the incident a secret between Susan and himself.

"Susan's *my* daughter, too! You had no right keeping that information from me. Don't you trust your own wife, Douglas?"

"Of course I trust you, but I just thought that we could—"

"And look where your thinking got us," Maggie barged in. She was fuming mad.

"Look, Mag. I'm man enough to admit I was wrong, so let's don't get into a heated battle out here. Alright?" Doug again looked over toward Warderick Wells Cay. "You stay here. I'm going ashore to find that young lady...and when I do, I'm going to give her a piece of my mind." Doug climbed over *C'DOCKED'R*'s coaming and into the Achilles. A hefty pull on the starter cord cranked the inflatable's small outboard engine. Doug then uncleated the painter from *C'DOCKED'R* and shoved off, heading towards shore against a swift tidal flow. "I'll be back as soon as I find her," Doug shouted back at Maggie over the outboard's loud drone. "Don't worry. Everything will turn out fine."

But Doug knew everything would not be fine. The same burning question kept tossing around in his head. How did Susan do it without him knowing? How did she sneak the drugs ashore? This really bothered Doug because Susan's bathing suit was simply too revealing. Drugs would have made a tell-tale bulge beneath the flimsy material.

Doug then recalled a news article he'd once read about a woman arrested for smuggling cocaine into the country by stuffing a baggie of the powder up her vagina. Was it possible that Susan had also read that article and had filed it away in her memory bank for future use? Was his daughter that desperate for a high? He hoped not.

With *C'DOCKED'R* being the only boat anchored at Warderick Wells Cay, Rob figured his best chance of getting off the island and back to Florida—his only chance—was aboard the sailboat. After explaining his predicament to Susan, she agreed, but warned that if her parents were to find out about his involvement with drug running, they would end their cooperation.

So, together, they thought up a way to get Rob a berth aboard *C'DOCKED'R* for the cruise back to Ft. Lauderdale. Rob insisted heavily that there were to be no lies in their explanation of the crash. He made Susan promise that everything they mentioned in their story to her parents would be the absolute truth, just not the whole truth. Susan agreed.

Satisfied with the details of their plan, Rob finally announced, "Let's get the hell outta here." Unsteadily, he stood up, using the fuselage against his back as a guide. "And Susan," he added.

"Yeah?"

"Thanks."

"What for?"

"For trusting me. Even if your folks suspect something and turn me in to the feds, thanks for trying."

Susan stared at Rob oddly. "You sound like you

don't think they're gonna believe us."

"The possibility's there, Susan. I'm hoping it doesn't come down to that, but if it does, I've got to face it. What else can I do? I can't stay here on Warderick Wells forever."

Not having anything to add to Rob's statement, Susan rose to her feet, braced Rob's right arm around her neck and walked him down the sloping wing to the sandy beach, where they began their slow trek across the island.

After rounding a bend about a half mile from the wreck site, Susan spotted her father. "Daddy! Over here!"

Doug hurried up the hill to Susan's side and took Rob from her arms. "What happened?"

"Daddy, this is Rob. He's a pilot and his plane crashed last night and he was trapped inside so I helped him get out. I was bringing him back to *C'DOCKED'R* with me so you could fix him up. He's hurt bad."

"Yes, I can see that," Doug acknowledged as he examined Rob's forehead. Not only was Doug relieved that Susan wasn't stoned, he was quite proud that she had been humanitarian enough to help someone in distress. Maybe he *had* been right about the cruise. Maybe it *had* done Susan some good. "Are there any others?" he asked while gently sitting Rob down on a nearby rock.

"There's another pilot and one passenger, but they're both dead, daddy."

"I'm sorry," Doug consoled Rob.

"Thanks." It was all Rob could think of to say.

"By the way, I'm Doug Baker. I assume Susan's already told you I'm a physician."

"Yeah, and it's the first piece of good luck I've had in months." With Dr. Baker still checking out the impact wound on Rob's forehead, Rob told him, "I think I've got a concussion. Every once in awhile, things go fuzzy on me."

"That's normal in a case like this. You shouldn't suffer any permanent damage, though, except for a nice scar above your left eye. And the fuzziness should clear up after a few days." Doug added, "This gash is fairly deep. I can suture it on the boat."

"Stitches?"

"It won't hurt."

"I've never had them before," Rob admitted awkwardly.

"Daddy only hurts a little," Susan teased.

"Thanks for the warning."

Next, Doug attended to Rob's leg injury—the cut above his right ankle. Eyeing the tourniquet, he commented. "Nice work."

"Susan did it."

"I'm even more impressed." Doug looked up at his daughter, then returned his attention to Rob's leg. "Susan's never shown any interest in my work."

"Your daughter's a life saver, Dr. Baker."

"Call me Doug. Okay, Rob?"

"Sure."

Doug's diagnosis of Rob's self-inflicted wound was good. The slice appeared worse than it really was. He prescribed a thorough cleansing, some antibiotic ointment applied generously to the wound and a sterile bandage change three times a day. Humorously, Doug asked Rob, "Where else does it hurt besides the obvious?"

Rob raised his swollen right hand. "It's broken bad. I can tell you that for sure. It hurts like a son of a —" he cut himself short.

"I get the picture," Doug said, smiling at Rob's sensitivity to Susan's presence. He lightly probed Rob's hand. "From the amount of swelling, I'd say there's a good chance of some major bone fractures. But without an X-ray machine, I can't be certain."

"I understand. Is there anything you can do, though, until I can get it X-rayed?"

Doug thought for a moment. "Perhaps I can!" he answered. "I've got a fiberglass repair kit aboard *C'DOCKED'R* that just might do the trick in making an improvised cast."

"Sounds good."

"Any other internal injuries...neck...chest...abdomen? Any spitting up of blood?" Doug went through the list routinely, as if Rob was in his office.

"None of that," Rob answered quietly. He was starting to get fuzzy again.

"You're a lucky man, Rob. Where are you from?"

"Florida."

"Oh, so are we! Isn't that a coincidence. We're from Ft. Lauderdale."

"I know. Susan told me. She said you have a real nice home on a waterway with a dock out back...and a pool." All Rob could think about now was water. He was so extremely thirsty. Looking skyward, he saw that what had been blue sky fifteen minutes earlier, was now a layer of thick, ominous clouds rolling in from the west—the cold front. He could feel the wind shifting directions. He asked Doug, "Shouldn't we be getting to the boat? I mean, I don't know anything about sailing, but as a pilot, I know that this system is going to break open real soon."

"You're absolutely right," Doug agreed. "I was so caught up in your injuries, the storm completely slipped my mind. Susan, help me lift Rob, please."

With Susan on Rob's right and Doug on his left, they lifted him off the rock. As they walked along the path, tiny droplets of rain began to fall. Cool rain. They quickened their pace the best they could without causing Rob additional pain. The Achilles was still some distance away.

As Doug motored out to *C'DOCKED'R* in the Achilles with Susan and Rob as passengers, the rain increased in strength, pelting down upon them in chilling streams. Rob opened his mouth and enjoyed his first drink of water in more than twenty-four hours. He bathed his face, washing away the dried blood. Despite being chilled, he felt refreshed and alive. He was going home to Florida.

Doug instructed Susan, "As soon as we're aboard, I'll need you to help me lash the inflatable to the foredeck. Then, I'm making it your responsibility to secure the companionway hatch while I take care of Rob in the main cabin."

Upon reaching *C'DOCKED'R*, Susan tied the Achilles' painter to a stern cleat, then flipped down the sailboat's transom-mounted ladder. She went up first, then turned around and helped ease Rob into *C'DOCKED'R*'s cockpit. Doug covered Rob from behind, then went up the ladder himself.

Doug shouted to Maggie, who was warm and dry in the sailboat's main cabin, "Open the hatch and help our guest below. Susan and I will be down in a few minutes."

When the hatch slid open and the boards were removed, Susan pointed Rob towards the companionway. She then climbed back down the transom ladder into the Achilles, unbolted the outboard and handed it up to her father, who affixed the small two-cycle engine to a wooden block mounted on *C'DOCKED'R*'s stern pulpit.

After again making her way up the ladder, Susan uncleated the painter and pulled the Achilles forward alongside *C'DOCKED'R*'s hull. Her father met her on the foredeck. Working in unison, they lifted the inflatable out of the water and over the starboard lifelines, turned it upside down and lashed it to the deck with nylon line. The rain was hard upon their backs, the wind fierce and biting.

With the inflatable in place, Doug and Susan hurried back to the cockpit, finding shelter beneath the bimini top. Both were dripping wet and cold. Doug went down the companionway first, quickly followed by Susan.

"Baby, I need you to—" But Doug was interrupted before he could finish his sentence.

"I know, daddy. You don't have to tell me again."

"Out of habit," he apologized, while Susan replaced the boards and secured the hatch. Doug immediately issued Maggie a set of instructions. "I'll need both of my medical bags and the boat's first aid kit, sterile gloves, a bowl of cleansing solution and a large stack of clean towels. I'll be back as soon as I change into something dry." Doug then stepped into the after cabin and shut the teak-trimmed door behind him.

Briefly, he reappeared to say, "Oh, and I'll also need the fiberglass repair kit. It's in the first drawer by the radio equipment. And I'll need some plastic wrap, too." Then, again, he disappeared into the cabin, closing the door.

Maggie went about her chore diligently, gathering up the needed items for her husband, all the while wondering anxiously what on earth was going on. The last thing she knew, Doug had gone ashore in seach of Susan, who was supposedly doing drugs. So who was this injured man they had brought back with them? And had Doug mentioned the word *guest*? Maggie neatly placed all of Doug's supplies over on the port settee, next to where their *guest* was sitting.

When Doug came out from his cabin, he was dressed in a warm, loose-fitting outfit. A robe was draped over his shoulder. "Here," he offered to Rob, handing him the robe. "This should be easy enough for you to slip into. You can dry off and change in the forward cabin." Then, pulling a towel off the stack Maggie had brought, he said, "Take this, too. I'll meet you right here when you're ready. Take your time."

"Thanks." Rob limped down the cabin sole, making his way the best he could to the forward cabin.

"When do I get to change?" Susan pouted, upset that Rob was getting all the attention. Her clothes were locked in the forward cabin with Rob.

"Have patience," Doug insisted.

But patience was something Susan didn't have. Grabbing two towels off the pile, she wrapped one around her waist, the other around her chest. She then wandered into the galley to get a can of soda from the icebox.

With Susan away from the settee, Maggie whispered to Doug, "Was she high?"

Shaking his head negatively, he answered, "Perfectly straight, Mag. No hint of drug use whatsoever." Doug then told Maggie as much as he knew about Rob and how Susan had helped him out of the wreckage.

CHAPTER SEVENTEEN

Sunday evening
   Doug spent the better part of two hours tending to Rob's injuries. Talk between them was light and friendly. It seemed they had a lot in common—sort of. They both loved nature and the outdoors. Though sailing and flying were different, each had similarities to the other. Common terms, common knowledge. Navigation principles were understood by both men. It was good talk.
   Maggie, meanwhile, had passed the hours preparing a hearty seafood dinner for four—stuffed yellowtail sauteed in butter, fried plantains and fresh-baked beer-bread. Susan had helped with the bread, sampling the beer in the process.
   With the hatches and portholes all closed off, the two-burner propane stove had made *C'DOCKED'R*'s interior a bit toasty, despite the six dorades being open. So, it was to everyone's relief when the rain finally stopped just as they were sitting down for dinner. Within minutes, the boat was opened up, aired out and cooled down. They were lucky—the afternoon forecast had been calling for rain all night.
   Doug switched on the radio and tuned it to the latest

marine broadcast for the area. He listened intently to hear if the end of precipitation had just been a fluke from the earlier forecast. It wasn't. The front had rained itself out. The rest of the broadcast, however, was still unpleasant. Winds were blowing out of the west-northwest at eighteen knots, with occasional gusts as high as twenty-six. Seas were running six to eight feet in open waters, choppy in the bays. The temperature had already dropped more than twenty degrees since frontal passage, with early morning lows expected in the low-fifties—quite nippy for the islands. Doug turned off the radio.

The meal was eaten quickly by all, mainly because nobody had eaten lunch. After dinner, with everybody sitting around the dinette, warm conversation filled the air. Soft light flickered about their faces from a gimbaled oil-lamp.

Rob felt good, as if his heart was expanding. Suddenly, he thought of the letter. A serious expression came across his face. He spoke up, calling everyone's attention to himself. Then, he remained quiet for half a minute, collecting his thoughts. He wanted to say something, but he wanted to say it right.

Susan gazed into Rob's eyes intently, thinking he was going to blow his cover. She held tightly, not wanting to believe that Rob would do something so dumb. Her parents would turn him in for sure.

Maggie touched Rob's arm gently, motherly. "Go ahead," she said in a soft feminine voice, "We're listening."

"I know you are, but it's hard for me. I'm not a very open person." Rob waited another minute, then began with, "Something's happening inside of me. I don't know what it is or why it's happening, but I can't deny it." Rob stared at each of the Bakers individually. First he looked across at Doug, then over at Susan, who was sitting next to him. Finally, he gazed at Maggie. Then he continued, "I guess what I'm trying to say is that I'm feeling all choked up inside, but in a good way. You're all treating me so nice...the doctoring, the kindness...and you don't even know me." Rob looked across at Maggie intensely and said, "That supper you made was one of the best meals I've ever eaten."

"Your compliment is graciously accepted." Maggie turned to her husband and teased, "It's good to know that somebody—" But she was interrupted before she could finish her sentence.

"Please, Mrs. Baker. I don't mean to be rude or anything, but let me finish what I've got to say. You don't know how long it's been since I've expressed feelings for other people. This is real important for me right now." Before starting again, Rob drank from a full glass of water, easily swallowing half a glassful down his throat. "I was just...I was...*damn!*" Rob lost his train of thought. "Where was I?"

"Relax," Doug offered. "Nobody's pressuring you here. Take your time. Suck in a deep breath of ocean air."

Rob took Doug's suggestion. It worked. Feeling better, he poured out his guts. "My life's a big, depressing mess. This past week has been especially bad for me."

Biting her nails, Susan thought for sure that Rob was going to blow his cover.

But Rob did not blow his cover. What he blew were his innermost personal feelings. "I don't like myself," he started off. "In fact, I hate myself. You may think I'm crazy for saying that, but it's true. I hate myself because of all the things I've done in the past. I've hurt a lot of people. Not physically, but emotionally. Last Monday night...the girl I love walked out on me because I wouldn't admit to her that I loved her. I don't ever wanna do that again...so that's why I'm telling you thanks for making me feel special. That's all I wanna say."

"That's it? I thought you were—" Susan shut her mouth before *she* blew his cover. She smiled at Rob, then asked, "What's her name...your girlfriend? The one who walked out on you?"

"Maureen." Rob almost choked saying her name. It had been difficult for him bringing her out into the open.

"Is she pretty?"

Maggie noticed Rob's eyes getting watery. "Susan, perhaps we should change the subject."

"No...it's okay, Mrs. Baker," Rob put forth. Turning to Susan, he answered, "Maureen's very pretty. And smart. She goes to college. She wants to be a teacher."

"Are you angry that she left you?"

"I don't blame her. It was my fault. I don't know what she ever saw in me anyway."

"Yeah, but if you love her, can't you two make up? Aren't you gonna see her when you get back home?"

The mention of home brought visions of the letter back into Rob's mind. He couldn't hold back his emotions any longer. With tears meandering down his face, he excused himself from the group, went into the forward cabin and shut the door behind him.

"Now see what you've done!" Maggie scolded Susan.

"I'm sorry, okay?" Susan really did feel bad that she made Rob cry. Wanting to apologize, she slid out of the dinette and followed Rob's path to the cabin. She reached out for the door knob, but did not turn it. Maybe Rob wanted to be alone, she thought. So, instead of entering the cabin, Susan turned and went into the head to be alone and to change her tampon. She cursed her period for always starting while she was on the boat.

Doug and Maggie were alone in the dinette. They looked at each other. It was Maggie who spoke first. "I wish there was something we could do for Rob. He seems like such a nice young man."

Doug thought awhile, then sprang to his feet. "There is something we can do, Mag. And right this minute!" He paced over to his navigation station, where a VHF marine radio was mounted to the underside of a cabinet. He lifted the mike off its hook.

"Who are you calling?"

"The Coast Guard. I was thinking...if they have a cutter plying these waters, they can pick Rob up tonight and rush him back to the mainland. I was planning to place the call in the morning, but why make Rob suffer any longer than he has to. His hand needs to be X-rayed and recast...and solid bedrest wouldn't be a bad idea to help ease his concussion. I've done all I can for him out here."

Susan came out of the head just as her father was bringing the mike to his lips. "Who's daddy calling?" she asked her mother.

"The Coast Guard, dear. He wants them to take Rob to a hospital tonight if possible."

"*No!*" Susan shouted as she ran over to her father, uncoupled the mike cord from the radio with her left hand, while prying the mike away from her father with her right. She then ran with the mike to the forward cabin, swung open the door and pounced onto the V-berth next to Rob. "Daddy was gonna call the Coast Guard, but I stopped him in time. I remembered what you said." Susan was crying. She knew she had blown Rob's cover. But she had no choice.

Doug and Maggie appeared in the narrow doorway leading to the cabin. "What's going on here?" Doug demanded to know.

Rob quickly pulled himself together. He couldn't blame Susan for what she had done—not after what he had told her about Falcon's network of informants. Rob knew the time had come to reveal the whole truth to Doug and Maggie—the truth about himself, the plane, the marijuana, Falcon, everything. He sat upright. "Don't be angry with your daughter. Susan was just trying to protect you...to protect all of us."

"For Christ's sake, from what?" Doug's arms were crossed in front of his chest as he leaned against the bulkhead.

"From death," Rob answered solemnly.

"*Death*? Did I hear you correctly?"

"Death," Rob repeated.

"Excuse me for appearing ignorant, but just how is my call to the Coast Guard going to cause...our deaths?"

"Because somebody's looking for me. For the plane, actually. If you call the Coast Guard and tell them about the crash, *that* somebody will hear about it almost immediately. He'll make the connection between the crash and me, and we'll all be dead before the Coast Guard can get a boat within five miles of Warderick Wells Cay. Believe me...*he can!*"

"I still don't understand. Why would he...this *somebody*...kill four people because of a plane crash?"

"Because the plane is his and it's full of marijuana. *His* marijuana."

"You're a smuggler!" Maggie gasped, nearly fainting.

"Ex-smuggler," Rob corrected. "Please let me explain." And he did just that, telling his miserable story in such detail that it took him almost an entire hour. His facial expressions reeked of honesty.

Maggie was not convinced. "You're still a smuggler, whether you say so or not. It's because of people like you that my daughter is a drug addict."

"No! You've got me pegged all wrong," Rob pushed

forth, standing his ground. "I never sold the stuff in my life. All I did was fly for Falcon. That's the truth."

"You expect me to buy those lies?"

"I don't expect you to buy anything, Mrs. Baker, but that's the truth."

"It is, mom," Susan insisted. "I wanted to take some pot off the plane, but Rob wouldn't let me."

"You keep out of this, young lady. I'll deal with you later."

"Calm down, Mag," Doug barged in with authority. "Let's be rational about this matter." Doug had believed Rob's story, for he had always been able to read into a person's sincerity. He turned to Rob. "Alright, let's say I believe you. What am I supposed to do now that my family is involved in this mess?"

"Well, there's two things you can do." Rob paused.

"Which are?" Doug was motioning with his hands for Rob to come out with it.

"One...you can put me ashore, sail away from Warderick Wells and forget about me. Let Falcon's people do what they want with me."

"I couldn't do that. It would be against my professional ethics. It would be murder."

"Then the only other thing you can do is to take me back to Florida aboard *C'DOCKED'R*. Once we're there, you can do whatever you want with me. Turn me over to the cops, the feds, whoever. Just promise me that you won't say anything over the radio. I'd never forgive myself if something happened to you and your family."

"I guess I have no other options."

"Then we have a deal? You'll take me?"

"Yes. We'll weigh anchor at sunrise."

Maggie stormed, "Are you out of your mind, Douglas? This man is a smuggler!"

"Ex-smuggler, Mag." And with that said, Doug told

the group, "Let's all get some sleep now. We've got a three to four day sail ahead of us, depending on the winds." Before retiring himself, Doug stayed to ask one last question of Rob. "Just to satisfy my curiosity...were you and Susan assuming right from the start that I was going to take you back to Ft. lauderdale?"

"Yeah."

"But that's ludicrous. The thought never entered my mind."

CHAPTER EIGHTEEN

Sunday night

Sleek, fast and sexy. If big toys were for big boys, then Rafael Ramairez's private jet was the ultimate image-maker. Packed with two turbofan engines, the white and blue aircraft rocketed at a cruising speed of 529 miles per hour. Costing three million plus, the jet was fully equipped, right down to its gold-plated ash trays, full wet-bar and VHS video system for inflight viewing of pornographic films.

The aircraft brought the world to Rafael's fingertips. All he had to do was dial one telephone number to get the action rolling. In the time it took Lucifer to chauffeur him in the Rolls Royce to Miami International Airport, his jet would be towed out of the hanger, fueled, iced and ready to go—anywhere, anytime. If Rafael wanted to fly south to Colombia, the flight was but a hop across the Caribbean Sea—a mere puddle jump for Rafael's plane.

Tonight's destination was Nassau in the Bahamas. Accompanying Rafael on the flight were Lucifer, Alec and two elegantly tailored call-girls. Fur coats kept the girls warm from the biting wind blowing across the airport ramp. With a price tag of $2,000 each per night, these girls were not everyday-variety street hookers.

Rather, they were the maximum in feminine pleasure machines, willing to fulfill any sexual fantasy a man—or woman— could possibly dream of.

Rafael had reserved the black girl for himself, allowing Alec to bed the fair-skinned beauty. Inter-racial sex was one of Rafael's greatest pleasures, second only to watching two women make love to each other. Tonight, in his Nassau residence, he would experience both.

After Rafael's two corporate pilots had loaded the baggage into the rear of the aircraft, he and his four guests boarded the plane. The two-piece door was closed and latched and, within minutes of engine spool-up, the jet was climbing ever higher over the Atlantic Ocean on its way to Nassau.

As soon as the seatbelt sign flashed off, both call-girls were on their knees, each taking a man into their mouth. The white girl quickly brought Alec to orgasm, pulling him out of her mouth just as he sprayed his hot liquid.

Alec moaned, "Angel, you've wasted me." He then slouched low in his seat, not bothering to stuff his softness back into his pants.

Rafael came shortly thereafter, depositing his load down the throat of the black girl. He smiled down at her. She smiled back. After she'd gotten up, Rafael turned to Alec, who was sitting beside him. "Are these ladies not what I promised?"

"And more!"

Rafael then signaled for both girls to go up front and service Lucifer. It was not like Rafael to share his ladies with his bodyguard, but tomorrow was Lucifer's birthday. "Happy Birthday, Lucifer," Rafael called out to his black companion.

Turning to look out the window, Rafael saw that the aircraft was flying above a milky cloud layer. Feeling the need for some *real* excitement—sexual thrills were never enough—he called his copilot on the jet's intercom and told him what he wanted.

"Stand by," replied the copilot. "I'll ask the captain."

Rafael threw his gaze forward. He could see into the cockpit, where the captain was nodding his head. Then the seatbelt sign flashed on.

The copilot came back over the intercom, "The captain acknowledges your request, Mr. Ramairez."

"How soon?" Rafael wanted to know.

"In about a minute, sir."

Rafael advised his four guests to secure their lapbelts. Since Lucifer had not yet reached orgasm, Rafael assured him there would be plenty of time for that later. The countdown was on.

When the minute was up, the captain of the jet—a Vietnam-era fighter jock—disengaged the plane's autopilot and manually eased the aircraft into a 360^0 roll to the right, pausing for a split-second in inverted flight. The feeling was sensational.

Once back in level flight, the captain asked for thumbs-up or thumbs-down and took a brief instant to look back into the cabin. What he got were six up's from his five passengers. The black girl had enjoyed the roll so much, she was holding up both her thumbs. So, with everyone's approval, the captain repeated the wild maneuver—this time around to the left.

The view of the harbor from Rafael's two-story Nassau residence was breathtaking. Looking out beyond the Paradise Island bridge from the balcony of the master bedroom, the city's lights emitted an almost day-like glow upon the water. The reflection was further enhanced by thousands of lightbulbs strung from bow to stern above two cruise ships berthed in port.

An even more spectacular sight, however, was the master bedroom itself. Decorated in pastel shades of pinks and mauves, the bedroom of Rafael's Bahamian hideaway had been designed with carnal thoughts in mind. The room's centerpiece was an antique brass bed encircled by sheer drapes. With its many rounded pillars of polished brass, the bed made an exquisite showcase for carrying out Rafael's bondage fantasies.

Directly opposite the bed were a pair of cushy chairs raised high off the floor on platforms, providing two excellent vantage points for watching the raw sexual exploits being performed on the bed's satiny sheets.

After turning on the stereo, Rafael climbed onto one of the chairs. Alec had already made himself comfortable on the other one. Lucifer was downstairs watching television. Not a word was exchanged between Rafael and Alec as they waited with pleasurable anticipation for the action to begin.

The girls knew exactly what was expected of them and each was eager to abide. It was the white girl, though, who took the initiative by removing the fur coat from her soon-to-be lesbian lover. She dropped the coat onto the plushly carpeted floor. Then, softly, she kissed the black girl with her glossy red lips, flicking her tongue within the warm confines of her lover's mouth.

Still embraced in a passionate kiss, the white girl somehow managed to shed her own fur. Then, reaching around behind herself, she unzipped her dress. After letting the dress fall to her ankles, she skillfully stepped out of it, never parting lips with the black girl.

Finally, the white girl could stand it no longer. Her heart racing with feminine desire, she ripped the dress off her sexual equal. Now, except for their high heels, garter belts and stockings, the two girls were totally naked in front of Rafael and Alec.

Not embarrassed by their sexuality, the girls explored each other's breasts—cupping, squeezing, kissing—until each had fully erect nipples. Their blood was boiling with passion. Ready to make serious love, they moved onto the bed. Then, lying down close to one another, they hugged their supple bodies into a warm endearing embrace.

Rafael was envious of the tenderness going on before his eyes. The sight of two women making love somehow seemed more natural to him than man and woman. Perhaps it was the way their soft skin intertwined with harmony as if each knew exactly what the other wanted. Whatever it was, Rafael never tired of the fantasy.

The girls grew bolder on the satin sheets, heightening their sexual feelings to new levels. Their petite muscles quivered with orgasmic spasms as their bodies played intimate games. Black on white. White on black. Woman on woman. Money could buy anything.

Alec had his eyes focused on the black girl as she licked the inner thighs of her female lover. Alec's mind, however, was somewhere else. He broke the silence between the two men. "Russ has had all day to gather intelligence on the plane, yet he still hasn't called."

"He'll call. He knows what's at stake. Russ owes the organization."

"I hope you're right." Alec thought intensely about the missing airfreighter while watching the black girl expertly swirl her tongue between the white girl's legs. Then, he said to Rafael, "I still think it was a well-planned rip-off by Rob and Nick. They could have refueled here in the islands and then flown the load up to the Carolinas...maybe even as far north as Maine. There's a lot of drug strips up that way now."

Becoming irritated at Alec's persistence, Rafael said

with all seriousness, "You're not thinking straight tonight, Alec. My associates in the Bahamas would never allow such an unauthorized landing...not without clearing it through me first."

"You do have enemies out here. Competitors, so to speak."

Taking his gaze off the girls and staring directly into Alec's eyes, Rafael insisted, "*No!* It was *not* a rip-off! That is why I am Falcon...because my instincts are as strong as those of the powerful bird of prey. I make it my purpose to know the people who work for me...to be ahead of them. I have been in this business for so long a time, Alec, only because I have remained sharp. That is where others have failed."

Rafael turned his attention back to the bed just as the white girl exploded with multiple orgasms. He counted at least a dozen separate contractions. He then said to Alec, "To end this brief discussion of ours, let us just say that when the plane is located, I want all of them taken out."

"Does *all* include Gustavo?" Alec questioned.

"All," Rafael assured him.

"But he is your nephew. You will have him killed?"

"I run a business, Alec. Profit and loss. Gustavo is a loss."

CHAPTER NINETEEN

Sunday night

Warderick Wells Cay was silent, cold and damp. The midnight wind howled throughout the downed airfreighter, entering through the cracked windshield, swirling past the bulkhead into the marijuana-laden cabin and finally channeling out the open emergency exits above each wing. The plane echoed a deadly resonance.

The coldness of the cockpit was enough to stir Gustavo, who was still impaled on the engine control levers, but on the verge of crossing into painful consciousness. When he finally emerged from the black depths, he immediately smelled the pungent odor of death. Although just barely able to sustain his own life, Gustavo's brain had enough cellular activity going on inside of it for him to function somewhat haphazardly. Lifting his head slightly to the right, he saw Nick's mutilated body strapped to the seat beside him. Decay had already festooned itself upon the dead copilot's injuries.

Gustavo then quickly looked to his left. His face turned acid red with hatred upon seeing the captain's seat empty. He swore to find and kill Rob—no matter what the personal cost to himself.

With purpose in his actions, Gustavo placed both

hands firmly on each side of the control quadrant, ready to free himself. In one great rush of adrenalin, he lifted his bodyweight upward, prying his chest loose from the multitude of control levers.

His shirt was a useless rag covered with body tissue and blood. Part of a broken rib was exposed, sticking out at an angle from his open chest wound. Pieces of torn skin hung like dripping molasses.

Then, planting both his feet onto the cockpit's metal decking, he unsteadily raised himself, reaching back to grip the bulkhead for support. Gustavo scanned for his gun, but found instead two forty-round clips of ammunition, which must have been blown from his pockets during the impact. Searching further, he finally found his MAC-10 automatic pistol underneath the copilot's right rudder pedal. It was a long reach for him and his body hurt from the awkward bending action, but he saw little choice in what he had to do. He needed firepower.

The MAC-10 was a formidable weapon in its automatic mode—and highly illegal. Able to empty a full clip in less than three seconds, the gun's reputation had made it the leading weapon of choice among smugglers. The MAC-10 was literally a portable handheld machine-gun.

Gustavo stashed the pistol into his waistband, turned to exit the cockpit, then stopped. He spun back around, drew his gun and, satisfying his ego, wasted an entire clip on Nick, shattering the silence of the night with automatic gunfire. "I remembers Houston!" Gustavo said out loud, not caring that he had used up forty good rounds on the already dead copilot.

Gustavo left the blood-stained cockpit, but found it difficult making his way up, over and around the bales. Without a flashlight, the aircraft's interior was pitch black. There were few shadows to help Gustavo decipher a path.

Eventually, though, he managed to find one of the emergency exits. In a hurry to climb out of the opening, he moved too quickly, stumbled and fell. The shock to his weakened heart caused the organ to go into palpitations.

Gustavo cringed from the pain. He massaged his chest for about a minute and a half before his heart finally steadied itself. Although the burning feeling was gone, he sat there resting on the floor, waiting awhile before mobilizing himself.

When he finally did get up, he climbed through the emergency exit with blood running through his thoughts—Rob's blood. Gustavo was eager to begin his manhunt, eager to track Rob down like an animal.

Sound had a peculiar way of traveling in the dead of the night, especially across deserted land and open water. Because of the rapidity of the bursts, Doug was finding it impossible to detect where the noise had originated or what it was.

Up until a few minutes ago, he and Maggie had been snuggled warmly under three blankets, asleep in *C'DOCKED'R*'s aft cabin. Now they were wide awake, sitting up in the double-berth.

Maggie gazed quizzically at her husband and suggested, "An engine backfire?"

"Possible, but I don't think so. Who would be cruising around in a boat this time of night? There's coral heads and shoals everywhere."

"Yes, but if they know the area, then it would be worth their risk if they were searching for something valuable."

"Like an airplane full of narcotics?"

"Yes."

"Are you suggesting Falcon's people are out here,

Mag?"

"Yes."

They were interrupted by a soft knock on the cabin's louvered door. "Is that you, Susan?" Doug called out.

"No. It's me," Rob whispered. "I've got to talk with you. It's important."

"Come in. The door's unlocked."

Rob entered the cabin, the glow from a small electrically-powered lantern illuminating his face. "Doug, you've got to sail us outta here now. Something's happened."

"The noise? Do you know what it was?"

"A gun...a MAC-10."

"See, Douglas!" Maggie screamed in anger. "I knew you should have called the authorities right away. Those drug people have already found the airplane and now they're looking for Rob. They must have fired the shots as a warning."

Doug asked Rob, "Could it be Falcon's people?"

"Who else would be firing a MAC-10 out there at this time of night? Gustavo is dead."

"You're sure of that...absolutely positive?"

"Yeah. What I don't understand is how the organization found the plane so fast? That's why you've got to sail us outta here tonight...like right now...before they spot the boat and figure out that I'm aboard."

Susan walked into the cabin, her palms rubbing the sleep from her eyes. "You woke me up. What's going on?"

"Quiet, Susan. Don't interrupt us." Doug continued with Rob, "You're sure the sound was gunfire?"

"Yeah. Automatic gunfire. I already told you...it was definitely a MAC-10. I've heard the sound enough times over the past year...down in Colombia at the airstrips. The guards were always shooting birds for target practice. And Gustavo fired his at Nick's feet just yesterday."

Doug swung his legs off to the side of the berth and slipped into a pair of long pants and a woolen sweater. Underneath, he was already wearing his thermal underwear. He knew it was inevitable that he attempt a nighttime departure—an extremely dangerous maneuver in the Bahamas. He left the cabin momentarily and went over to the main switch panel next to the navigation station. He turned off the switch to the masthead light, making *C'DOCKED'R* nearly invisible to anyone on shore. Then, upon re-entering the aft cabin, he grabbed a flashlight from a shelf, turned it on and shut off the cabin's electric lantern.

Doug told his wife and daughter, "You two better put on some warm clothing. We'll be getting underway very shortly." Doug then reached for his jacket, exited the cabin and headed up the companionway, praying he wouldn't run *C'DOCKED'R* aground or shear off the boat's keel on a coral head while motoring out of the anchorage. Fortunately for him, *C'DOCKED'R* was shoal draft.

Also fortunate for him—and for everyone aboard the sailboat—was the fact that the cold front had come through. Had it not been for yesterday's forecast, Doug would have anchored *C'DOCKED'R* off the western shore of Warderick Wells Cay, close to the shipwreck he and Susan had planned to explore. That would have made a nighttime departure impossible due to the perilously shallow waters of the Exuma Bank off the island's west side.

At least off the eastern shore of Warderick Wells, once cleared of the harborage area and then out past the northern tip of Hog Cay, *C'DOCKED'R* would have nothing but deep water beneath its keel. Exuma Sound was to be Doug's saving grace. From there, he could chart a safe course for the southern tip of Eleuthera Island. With the winds as they were, however—having shifted around to the northeast during the night—the sail was going to be a wet and sluggish beat to weather. Doug prayed for the best.

CHAPTER TWENTY

Monday morning
 Rob could clearly hear the water's force pounding against *C'DOCKED'R*'s hull as he lay curled up in the fetal position on the V-berth, his eyes remaining tightly closed. Sailing was a new experience for him and his body's equilibrium had not yet adjusted to the myriad sensations of the sea. It was nothing like cruising around the Everglades in his bass boat.
 Feeling a bit queasy, he wondered if he would ever get used to the motion. Doug had said the sail back to Ft. Lauderdale would take three to four days. That was a long time to be seasick.
 Rob wished he could fall back asleep. It had felt so good. But he couldn't, so all he had to concentrate on was the constant pitching and rolling of the boat. He wondered what had woken him up in the first place. He knew he was still tired. Had it been the sound of birds flying overhead? Or was it the sailing commands he'd heard Doug shouting to Susan and Maggie—*ready about, lee ho* and all the rest of the strange new phrases? Everything seemed so foreign to Rob.
 Suddenly, his mind switched directions on him. He thought about Warderick Wells Cay, the crash, the air-

freighter stuffed with marijuana, Falcon's people searching the island for him with their MAC-10's ready to blow him away. Rob felt the hairs on his arms raise. He wondered how far away *C'DOCKED'R* was from the island.

Then, Rob sensed something—a presence of some sort. He felt as if someone was staring directly at him, as if somebody was witnessing him lying there in *C'DOCKED'R*'s V-berth. Was it because he'd been thinking about Falcon's gunmen? Was he going crazy? The feeling seemed so real—real enough for him to want to face whatever it was.

He knew he had to open his eyes. He had to prove to himself that his mind was only playing games in his head. He had to show himself that in reality there was nobody there in the cabin with him.

Rob had two choices in opening his eyes. He could open them quickly and get it over with. Or, he could allow his eyelids to slowly drift open, seeing first a hazy blurr of the cabin, followed by a more-in-focus view of his surroundings.

For some reason, he was scared. So, because of his fright, he chose the second approach. Keeping his right eyelid fully closed, he squinted through a sixteenth-of-an-inch slit created by his partially-opened left lid. Blurrily gazing across to the other side of the V-berth, he refused to believe what he was seeing as a human form filled his vision. His mind had to be playing tricks on him, he thought.

His body drenched with sweat, Rob decided to be brave about the whole thing. He opened wide both his eyes. There, sitting across from him, smiling, was Susan. Rob was relieved.

"Hi, Rob. You missed breakfast." She was wearing the same black bikini as yesterday.

"What time is it?" he asked.

"Quarter of ten. And it's a beautiful day. The clouds are gone. The sun's up. The air was chilly until about eight o'clock, but now the temperature's warmed up to almost seventy. That's probably why you're sweating so much. You don't need all those blankets anymore. Mom covered you up with them last night after me and daddy carried you in here. You passed out."

"I passed out?"

"Yeah. You don't remember."

"No." Rob sat up in the berth, trying to brush his tossled hair with his left hand, but couldn't because of the bandages wrapped around his head. "Do you have any aspirin?" he asked.

"Sure. I'll go get some," Susan offered cheerfully. She hurried into the main cabin, popped a couple of aspirin into her hand from the medical supply kit and brought them back to Rob, along with a glass of orange juice.

"I don't drink juice," Rob said apologetically.

"Really? I thought everyone liked juice."

"Not me."

"Are you a picky eater, too?"

"Yeah. Name some foods you think everybody likes," Rob joked.

"Pizza," Susan suggested. Surely Rob must eat pizza, she thought.

"Nope."

"Okay, how about spaghetti?"

"Not me."

"Are you serious? You don't like pizza or spaghetti?"

"I swear." He was telling the truth.

"God, what do you eat, then?"

"Meat and potatoes...french fries only, though. *And green beans.*"

Susan was amazed. "That's all you eat?"

"Basically, so just get me a glass of water for the pills and I'll be fine, okay?"

"Sure." Susan scampered off again, this time returning with a glass of cold water.

Rob swallowed the two aspirin tablets and chased them with water, then handed the empty glass to Susan. "So what happened to me last night? Why'd I pass out? Did your dad say if it was because I was seasick?"

"That's what started you off. *C'DOCKED'R* was pitching pretty good. I guess it got to your stomach right away."

"Yeah, my stomach's still not feeling all that great."

"Anyway, it was pretty cold outside when we left the anchorage. You stayed below 'cause all you were wearing was daddy's robe. I guess it didn't take you long before you got seasick. You made a thud when you fell 'cause when I stuck my head in the hatchway to see what the noise was, you were face down on the cabin sole. Daddy tried bringing you around with ammonia, but you were out of it. He said your concussion had something to do with it and that sleep was the best thing for you, so we carried you in here."

"Your mom's pissed that your dad's going through all this trouble for me, isn't she?"

"Yeah. I think there's gonna be a big fight when we get home."

"I didn't mean to start anything between them. All I wanna do is get back to Florida."

"You didn't start it, Rob. They've been fighting for months."

"Yeah, but that's not the point. I just wish your mom would believe me like your dad does. Everything I've said *has* been the truth."

"Don't worry about mom. She's a marshmallow

around daddy. He always gets his way."

"I guess it's good that he's the one who trusts me, then." Rob studied the cramped quarters of the forward cabin. He said to Susan, "Your dad's got a nice boat. A little tight in here, but cozy."

"Yeah. *C'DOCKED'R*'s good for cruising the Bahamas. We used to have a smaller sailboat...a twenty-two footer named *DREAMER*...but daddy traded up a couple years ago. Now he's talking about trading up again."

Changing the subject, Rob asked, "How far are we from Warderick Wells?"

"Still a little nervous about those people with the guns?"

"I guess."

"Well, you don't have to worry about them anymore. I'll show you exactly where we are on a chart a little later." Susan all of a sudden started laughing.

"What's so funny?" Rob wanted to know.

"I was just thinking how those people must be going crazy trying to find you on that island."

"It's not funny, Susan. We're lucky to be alive. We're lucky they didn't—"

"You don't have to get mad at me," Susan barged in, not letting Rob finish. "I'm sorry for laughing, okay?"

"I'm not mad at you. Why do you keep thinking I'm mad at you?"

Ignoring Rob as if she'd already forgotten the conversation, Susan said, "Wait here. I've got something for you. I'll be right back." She left the cabin. Upon returning, Susan handed Rob fresh clothes. "Here. They're daddy's. There's a pair of shorts, a T-shirt and underwear. They should fit you. You're only a couple inches taller than him."

"I think I'll pass on the underwear," Rob said as he

gave them back to Susan.

"But they're clean."

He still refused.

"They won't bite you, Rob."

"Heh, I'm serious. I don't need them. Mine should be dry by now."

"And I guess you're gonna wear them for the next four days, too, right?"

"You're a persistent little bitch, aren't you?" Rob was smiling.

Susan laughed. "Yeah. And I'm just like daddy. I always get my way." She threw the briefs into Rob's lap.

Rob moved closer to the edge of the berth and rested his feet on the cool, teak sole. He glanced up at Susan, who was standing in the doorway.

She stared back at Rob and said, "Well, aren't you gonna get dressed?"

"And aren't you gonna leave the cabin?"

She didn't answer him. Instead, Susan brazenly sat down on the berth opposite Rob, not taking her eyes off him.

"Is something wrong?" Rob asked in bewilderment.

"No. I just think you're cute, that's all."

"Well, don't look so goo-goo-eyed." Rob was in no mood to have a sixteen year old girl romancing him, especially when her parents were so close at hand.

"Goo-goo-eyed?" Susan chuckled.

Rob was embarrassed—another new emotion for him. Not knowing how to handle the emotion, he put up a defense barrier. "Hell, I don't know what word you kids use today."

"It's certainly not goo-goo-eyed," Susan laughed again. "And I still think you're cute, even though you think I'm a kid, which I'm not."

With his defenses still in force, Rob said, "I'd like to

get dressed now." He pointed for her to leave the cabin.

"Can't I stay and watch?"

"No!"

"Why not?"

"Because why would you wanna do that, anyway?" He had no idea what kind of an answer he'd get from Susan.

"'Cause you've got a sexy body and I like looking at sexy bodies. That's why."

Frustrated from Susan's sexual teasing, Rob insisted, "Stay if you want. See if I care."

But Susan was sharp and caught on immediately. "You're trying to fake me, aren't you? You think I'll chicken out and leave. Well, I won't. I've seen cock before."

"Do your parents know you talk like this?"

"Yessssss!" she hissed, as she closed the door with her legs. Susan reached up and locked the door to get Rob's reaction.

At this point, Rob didn't care anymore. If Susan wanted to stay, then let her stay. He was tired of playing her games and didn't give a damn how much she saw. He stripped out of the robe in front of Susan's watchful eyes, stepped into the briefs and pulled them up to this waist, then pulled on the green nylon shorts. The fiberglass cast on his right hand and forearm caused him problems only when he tried getting the T-shirt on over his bandaged head.

Susan watched the ripples move across Rob's muscular chest as he struggled with the T-shirt. Her main attention, however, was on the black charm dangling from the golden chain hanging around Rob's neck. She'd first noticed the black bird yesterday at the crash site when she'd removed Rob's shirt to make the tourniquet.

The smooth charm disappeared from Susan's view

as Rob finally managed to pull the T-shirt over his head. Susan asked him, "You think I'm a prick-teaser, don't you?"

"Shit, who wouldn't."

"I'm not."

"Then why don't you give me a break and lighten up a bit. My mind's not on sex...especially not with you."

"Okay, I'll stop. But don't be mad at me."

"There you go again. Why do you keep saying that?"

"I don't know. I guess I keep thinking you are. And I'm *really not* a prick-teaser. Me and my boyfriend have sex all the time."

"Jesus Christ, Susan! Just drop it already, okay?"

And she did. "Does that charm you're wearing have anything to do with Falcon? You know...the bird with the pot leaf?"

"It's supposed to be a symbol of obedience. Sort of a mental handcuff."

"Then you don't need it anymore."

"Right."

"Can I have it as a souvenir?"

Rob reached into the shirt, but changed his mind and withdrew his hand. "No," he answered rather bluntly.

"But why? I thought you couldn't wait to be free from Falcon."

It was a good question and Rob thought it over for a long time. Why didn't he want to part with the black falcon? After all, he was off the island and heading back to Florida. He searched his brain for an answer, but finally resigned himself to the fact that he didn't have an answer. He told Susan, "I just have this weird feeling that now's not the time to get rid of it."

"That doesn't make sense."

"I know." For the first time, Rob realized what a

strong psychological bond the black falcon charm had on him. He also realized it was going to take a lot of soul-searching to break the bond.

Sensing that Rob no longer wanted to talk about the charm, Susan asked, "How's your stomach doing?"

"Better than before. At least I'm not feeling nauseous now. I think I might even be getting used to the boat's motion a little."

"You want something to eat, then? Lunch won't be for a couple more hours."

"Okay. How about a piece of toast...and two scrambled eggs?"

"You've got 'em."

CHAPTER TWENTY-ONE

Monday afternoon
With a stiffened breeze, the sailing was exhilarating as *C'DOCKED'R* sliced to windward off the eastern shore of Eleuthera Island under reefed main and working jib, close-hauled on a starboard tack. Doug was driving the boat hard. He was glad *C'DOCKED'R* had a steady helm as the sloop raced along at six and a quarter knots, its port rail in the water.

The wave action had also picked up its rhythm over what it had been earlier. *C'DOCKED'R* rose majestically with each approaching roller, pointing skyward as if wanting to fly. Then, with salt spray and foam whipping back over the bow, the sloop would break through the watery crest, only to face earth's gravitational pull, which would bring the boat crashing back down the backside of the wave—only to be followed by the next wave.

It was a gorgeous day to be outdoors, a perfect afternoon to be sailing the crystalline waters of the Bahamas. The cold front had cleared the air and not a cloud was seen in the deep-blue sky. Here was paradise found.

As far as cruising grounds went, the Bahamas offered everything. Beautiful and protected anchorages abounded and activities for the avid sportsman were unending. There was deep-sea fishing, scuba diving, water skiing, wind surfing and parasailing. But that was not all. The list went on. For those not so inclined to physical exertion, there was shell collecting, nature walks, bird watching and cave exploring. For the uninhibited, nude sunbathing on the white powdery sands of a secluded beach was at its best in the Bahamas. Truly, the islands were a tropical paradise.

Doug thought about the past week, having once again enjoyed the area's "out-island" charm. As always, he would miss the Bahamas once home. Then he thought about Rob and wondered why he hadn't come up on deck. Doug called below, telling Rob the fresh air would do him some good. After a few minutes, Doug saw movement in the companionway. It was Rob. "Well, I see somebody had a very good sleep."

Rob jutted his head out the hatch. "Hi." Doug was right, he thought. Down below was not the place to be on a sailboat. The fresh air felt relieving as it brushed his unshaven face. "I hope I wasn't too much trouble last night."

"Not at all. It can happen to anyone. Even to an experienced sailor."

Rob stepped out into the cockpit and sat down between Maggie and Susan, leaning his back against the starboard coaming. Doug was a couple feet over, sitting center-line behind the round, stainless-steel wheel.

There was a land mass in the distance, but the island was too far away for Rob to make out any specific details. It was maybe five or six miles off to port, he estimated. He turned to Doug. "Is that Eleuthera over there? Susan was showing me your charts before."

Doug acknowledged Rob's inquiry and added, "The RDF was indicating Rock Sound directly abeam

C'DOCKED'R half an hour ago."

Rob shook his head in understanding. He knew where Rock Sound was. He'd once flown a load of hotel supplies to the airport there—napkins, paper towels and the like.

Doug added, "We're logging fairly decent progress today."

"What about tonight?" Rob asked out of curiosity. "Have you picked a habor yet? A safe one where the chance of somebody spotting us is small?"

"Don't have to. We're sailing right on through to Chub Cay in the Berry Islands via the Northeast Providence Channel. We'll make a brief stop there before continuing on our way to Florida. I've set up a schedule of alternating watches between Maggie, Susan and myself. There will always be two of us on deck and we'll catch sleep during our off-watch hours."

"Straight through...you mean like all night?"

"Yes. It's about a day and a half to two day sail to Chub Cay. I'm estimating Wednesday morning."

"What about me, then? Can't I help out?" Rob was observing the ease at which Doug was steering *C'DOCKED'R* with his feet propped up on the wheel. He offered, "I'm sure I can learn to steer the boat."

"Oh, I don't doubt you, Rob. But I'd rather you didn't. It's in your best interest not to concentrate on anything too strenuous right now." Doug was leaning back against the stern pulpit. Occasionally, he would lean forward and glance at the compass mounted on the steering pedestal.

"What's so tough about what you're doing?" Rob questioned. "You look the most relaxed of any of us."

"I'm talking about mental stress, Rob. A concussion shouldn't be taken lightly. You know what happened to yourself last night. Concentrating on holding

C'DOCKED'R on course would be too much for you. It would give you a headache. It's second nature to me."

"Yeah, but I feel like a freeloader...somebody just bumming a ride. That's not my way. I want to earn my ride. There's got to be something I can do."

"Just enjoy the cruise."

For no apparent reason, Maggie suddenly broke out in laughter—sarcastic laughter.

"A private joke, Mag?"

"Cops and robbers," was all Maggie said, still smirking beneath her breath.

"Excuse me?" Doug looked puzzled.

"It's just that I finally figured out what you're doing, Douglas. You're living out your childhood memories, the excitement of it all, playing cops and robbers. Only you've chosen the wrong side and you've involved your family."

"Talk some sense, Mag."

She continued, "Don't you see? It's all going to blow up in your face...at Chub Cay."

"Nothing's going to happen at Chub Cay, Mag. When have we ever had a problem at Chub Cay? Never...that's when."

By the tones of their voices, Rob realized his presence aboard *C'DOCKED'R* had something to do with the talk about Chub Cay. He remembered too, that Doug had mentioned something about making a short stop-over at the island. "I take it I'm involved in this mess."

"You are," Doug agreed.

"So what's gonna happen at Chub Cay?"

"Mag's a little excited, Rob. Nothing's going to happen at Chub—" A powerful gust of wind came roaring out of the east, catching Doug by surprise. The sloop heeled violently well beyond safe limits. Reacting instinctively, Doug released the mainsheet while turning the wheel hard to windward. Immediately, the sailboat's angle of heel decreased as *C'DOCKED'R* rounded up into the wind.

Doug had managed a glimpse of the electronic windspeed indicator during the gust. In a matter of seconds, the wind had jumped from a brisk twenty-one knots all the way up to thirty-three. Then, just as quickly as the gust had appeared, it was gone.

The wind was now down to a steady twenty-two, but blowing a tad more easterly than before the gust. Doug brought *C'DOCKED'R* back on course and retrimmed the sails, this time on a close-reach. A look at the knotmeter told him a fractional unit of speed had been gained in the sailboat's quest for the Northeast Providence Channel.

"What was that all about?" Rob wanted to know.

"Just one of nature's tricks to contend with at sea. Did it scare you?"

"A little."

"Well, it was nothing really."

"Oh." Rob then reminded Doug, "You were saying about Chub Cay."

"Yes. All that's going to happen at Chub is that I'm clearing out with Bahamian Customs there. It's standard procedure...routine. I have to turn in the boat's transire and my family's immigration cards."

"Customs?" Rob had thought he was home-free, but now he wasn't so sure. "What about me? I don't have any papers. What if they start asking questions?"

"They won't, Rob. I assure you of that. They won't even know you're aboard. You'll go below into the forward cabin on our approach to Chub and stay down there until after I've cleared Customs and you won't come up until the island is well astern of *C'DOCKED'R*."

"Yeah, but what if they search the boat? What then?"

"They won't do a vessel search. Not at Chub Cay. That's why I chose it over Bimini. Trust me."

"How can I? How can you be so sure Customs won't board *C'DOCKED'R*?" Rob asked excitedly. "I'm not stupid. I know searches are random." Then, accusingly, before he even gave Doug the opportunity to explain, Rob added, "You're turning me in to the Bahamians, aren't you? You were planning it all along."

"Hold it right there. You're not being fair to me, Rob. Up until now, I've put my absolute trust in you. From this point on, you're just going to have to do the same for me. When I said I'd take you back to Florida, I meant it."

Rob wanted to apologize to Doug, but he didn't know what to say. Looking out to sea, he regressed for a few minutes into a world of his own, his thoughts hidden deep. Then, still looking out upon the ocean, he let out a soft, "I'm sorry. I shouldn't have—" Rob paused. After collecting his thoughts, he started over. "I know I shouldn't have said what I said. Especially since you have every right to turn me in if you want to. But the thought of going to a Bahamian jail where I'd be tried, found guilty and put out to dig ditches all within a twenty-four hour period...I guess it just made me a little crazy for a second. I'm sorry." Rob then turned to face Doug. "I'm sorry," he said for the third time.

"Apology accepted. Now let me explain to you exactly what is going to happen at Chub Cay. There's this cove at Chub Point where we'll drop anchor. Maggie and Susan will remain aboard *C'DOCKED'R* while I, alone, will take the Achilles over to the dock. There, I'll catch a ride up the road to the airport, where the Customs house is located. You, of course, will still be below in the cabin. I shouldn't be at the airport for more than fifteen minutes at the most if the Customs officials are there...which sometimes they're not, but no matter. Anyway, I'll have all the proper documentation and paperwork with me, so there'll be no reason for them to come out to the boat to perform a vessel search. In fact, never in the twenty-odd years I've been cruising to the Bahamas have I ever been boarded while clearing out at Chub Cay. The Customs officials there don't like hassling with the ride from the airport to the dock and then out to the anchorage."

Susan butted in, "But mostly it's 'cause daddy always brings them a case of beer."

Ignoring his daughter's comment, Doug finished by telling Rob, "Clearing out at Chub Cay will be a very relaxed affair. It would be a different story if we were clearing out at Bimini, but only slightly. There, *C'DOCKED'R* would have to be tied up to a dock within walking distance of the Customs house, making the chance of an arbitrary boarding greater. Although, even in Bimini searches are rare. So, see how easy it is?"

"That's it?" Rob asked. "That's all that's gonna happen?"

"Nothing more. Guaranteed."

Rob stared at Maggie, then turned back to Doug. Pointing, he asked, "Then why did she make such a big deal about it...saying that everything was going to fall apart at Chub Cay?"

"I don't know."

Rob felt bad that he had also made a big deal about it. "I guess I made an ass outta myself, didn't I?"

"Only half an ass," Doug laughed.

CHAPTER TWENTY-TWO

Monday afternoon

It was quarter past four in the afternoon when Maureen left FIU's Bay Vista campus in her rusted-out Pinto. She headed up US-1 a short distance before turning west onto 163rd Street. A few miles down the road, after entering onto a serpentine maze known as the Golden Glades Interchange, her Pinto was forced to a standstill.

Up a way, maybe half a mile or so, a pair of cars had joined together in a tangle of bent metal, causing one of Miami's daily rush-hour traffic jams. Although the flashing blue lights meant police officers were already at the scene, the wrecker trucks hadn't yet arrived to haul away the damaged vehicles.

Progress was slow as several lanes jockeyed into single file. Human nature being what it was, forward movement was slowed even further as each driver took their turn to gawk at the accident as they passed the collision site.

Twenty-five minutes later, Maureen was again on her way, shooting west along the 826 Expressway. She was doing sixty-eight miles per hour in the little Pinto, which was really pushing the car. Normally, Maureen didn't speed, but Jackie had asked her to work the five to two shift at the bar—overtime on her only night off—and she wanted to at least drive home first to freshen up and change clothes.

By the time she pulled into the driveway of her apartment complex, it was already well past five o'clock. Maureen parked her car, walked over to a wall-mounted cluster of mailboxes and pulled out her mail, not bothering to sort through the envelopes. She raced up the stairs to the second floor, then ran down the hall about a third of the way to her door.

The apartment was tiny and of the studio variety, with the main living area doubling as a bedroom. While going to college, it was all the space Maureen needed, and with her simple decorating ideas, she'd turned her unit into a cozy, yet manageable home.

Once inside the apartment, Maureen dropped her keys, purse and mail onto the kitchen countertop, then headed straight for the bathroom, undressing along the way. She cleansed her face with a soapy washcloth, rinsed thoroughly and towel dried, afterwhich she sprayed Opium between her ample breasts and re-applied eye shawdow, mascara and lipstick.

After slipping into a pair of jeans and a pull-over top, Maureen went back into the kitchen and reached for her purse and keys. As she did, one of the envelopes on the countertop caught her attention. Although the envelope didn't have a return address written on it, Maureen knew exactly who it was from, for her name and address were clearly scribbled in Rob's sloppy handwriting.

Nervously, Maureen tore at the glued seal and pulled out the letter. It was a long letter, running four pages front and back. She began reading it, but found the meaning of Rob's first few paragraphs difficult to follow, almost as if he hadn't been too sure of himself when he'd written the letter. The writing seemed to go on forever.

Then, halfway into the second page, Maureen's knees went weak—so weak that she couldn't support her hundred and twelve pounds any longer and had to lower herself to the cold linoleum floor. Two watery streams gently flowed from the corners of her eyes. Rob's meaning was now clearly understood.

At each turn of the page, Maureen's tears increased in delicacy, for the more she read, the more the letter explained. It explained about Stacy, about the other women, about the whores. It explained about Rob's secret life as a drug pilot and about the Winnebago and about how he was going to use the motorhome to escape from the smuggling organization.

When Maureen turned to the last page, her eyes were drawn down to Rob's final paragraph and to his closing words.

> So that's why I wanted to tell you that I loved you when we were down there in Key West, but when you pressed me about it in the bar, I just couldn't face up to it. That's why I said "NO" when I really wanted to say "YES." And then, when you told me that we were through and you walked out on me, I totally lost it. I'm not blaming you, though. I want you to know that. I guess it's best this way anyhow, because you deserve better than me. And you probably wouldn't have come with me if I had asked. So take care of yourself and always stay pretty.
> Love,
> Rob
> P.S. Don't Hate Me!!!

"Bastard!" she screamed aloud. It was out of love that Maureen cursed Rob. She crumpled the letter into a wad and threw it furiously at the wall. Then, placing her head between her knees and her hands on top of her head, she sat there on the floor and cried, feeling extremely lonely. She cried for a long time. Her Key West ploy had backfired.

The same unanswerable questions kept rebounding in her mind—why? Why did Rob keep his love hidden from her for so long and then tell her about it in a letter? Why did he tell her in a way so that she could do nothing about it? If he really loved her, then why did he leave town without her?

Maureen wondered where Rob was? He'd only written that he was heading out of Florida. There was no mention of a destination. Was he in Georgia? Was he in Alabama? Suddenly, it came to Maureen that she'd skipped over most of the letter's last page. Maybe there was a hint of Rob's destination in the unread paragraphs.

She crawled across the kitchen floor over to the far wall and retrieved the wadded letter. Undoing her damage, she carefully opened the wad, then pressed the pages flat against the floor, smoothing out the wrinkles with her hands. Disappointment soon overshadowed her hopes, however, when the previously unread portion turned up not a single clue as to Rob's whereabouts.

Not wanting to believe that Rob would leave her this way, Maureen reshuffled the pages into sequential order and started over from the beginning, praying for an answer as she read. The writing seemed to go on forever, running four pages front and back. When she was finished, the truth hit her hard. She had lost Rob.

CHAPTER TWENTY-THREE

Monday night

Rafael rambled on, "Enliven your psyche, Lucifer. Delight your senses. It's good for your soul...for your mind. It's God's gift to mankind. I know this because God talks to me, Lucifer. So feast your nose again on God's mighty offering. Praise the Lord. Praise be He who giveth us this powerful substance."

Rafael, Alec and Lucifer had been snorting cocaine since before lunchtime—about eight hours hence—and were still at it. The three men were sitting around an exquisite crystal coffee table in the downstairs living room of Rafael's Bahamian hideaway. There were no girls to play with, just the unweighed mound of cocaine spread out on the table. The two prostitutes had been whisked back to Miami earlier in the afternoon aboard the jet.

Lucifer, being just as much a believer in the white angelic drug as his boss, reached into the mound and pinched a fair amount between his fingers. Not bothering to use a snorting tube, the black bodyguard brought his fingers up to his nose and inhaled the powdery drug into his inflamed nostrils. He licked the remaining traces of cocaine from his fingers.

Alec said to Rafael, "You treat this nigger too well."

"He is a trusted friend, Alec. Lucifer and I have been together a long time, just as you and I have." The phone rang. "Answer that, Alec."

The telephone was on the coffee table, but at the opposite end from where Alec was seated. He reached across both Rafael and Lucifer and lifted the receiver. "Hello?" Hearing the familiar voice, Alec placed his hand over the phone and informed Rafael, "It's Russ."

"I want results! He's had two full days."

Alec went back to the receiver. "Falcon wants results, Russ. What have you found for him? Good news, I hope...for your health's sake. He's losing faith in your high-sung promises."

"Yeah, well, tell Falcon his plane's been located. A Coast Guard C-130 on routine island patrol spotted the wreckage this afternoon during an over-flight of the Exuma chain. The airfreighter went down on Warderick Wells Cay. You familiar with the area?"

"Yes. What about the cargo? Who took control?"

"The Bahamian Defense Force impounded the stuff."

"You're sure of this, Russ?"

"Positive. My sources are good." Then Russ broke with the bad news. "Tell Falcon he's got a man on the loose. One of the pilots."

When the DEA man didn't offer more, Alec barked, "I need details, Russ!"

So Russ gave Alec details. "The Coast Guard was able to get some men ashore before the Bahamians got there. From what I can gather, they recovered two bodies. The first was found slumped over on the ground about two hundred yards down the beach from the plane's left wingtip. Latin male, mid-twenties, armed with a MAC-10, died of massive chest injuries. Part of his rib-cage was found on the engine controls, so they suspect he was riding jumpseat. The second body was pulled from the cockpit, right seat, caucasian male, close to sixty, but hard to tell due to severe head injuries, facial features beyond recognition. No trace of the left seater anywhere near the wreckage. A thorough search of the island produced negative results. Not even footprints. They think he somehow got off the island before the front passed through yesterday. The rain must have washed away the prints."

"Anything else?"

"That's all I've got."

"You let me know the minute you get wind of the captain turning up. I'll be at this number until tomorrow morning." Alec reached back across the coffee table and replaced the receiver. He looked at Rafael. "Gustavo and Nick are out of your worry."

"And Rob?"

"Missing." Alec then filled Rafael in on the situation down on Warderick Wells Cay.

Rafael's response to the information was businesslike. "I'll arrange a meeting tomorrow with my good friends in the Bahamian Parliament. They'll see to it that their government return to me what is mine."

"And Rob? What do we do about him?"

"Nothing, Alec. Let Rob make his way to Tampa. He will be well taken care of when he starts the motorhome."

CHAPTER TWENTY-FOUR

Tuesday evening

Tuesday had been a quiet day—a day of reflection, especially for Rob. After nearly two full days of non-stop sailing, everyone aboard *C'DOCKED'R* had pretty much settled into the routine of Doug's watch system.

The evening stars were out in full force above *C'DOCKED'R* as Maggie and Susan stood watch on deck, maintaining the boat on a westerly course down the Northeast Providence Channel. The winds had slackened during the latter part of the day and were now blowing out of the east at eleven knots.

Doug and Rob were below in the main cabin, sitting around the dinette enjoying after-dinner beers, talking about Rob's past.

When the conversation came around to Rob's involvement with Falcon's smuggling operation, Doug asked, "But didn't you ever think about the illegality of what you were doing?"

"Sure I did...all the time. But what could I do about it? Once I got involved, I knew too much. They forced me to continue. And I couldn't go to the cops. That's why I bought the motorhome...to get the hell away from everything."

"Right, but that was after you were already with the organization for quite some time. I still don't understand how you rationalized the drug flying when you first became involved?"

"It was easy, actually. I'd been working my ass off for years flying cargo runs out of Miami and not making much money at it. Then Gustavo offered me a hundred grand to make one flight down to Colombia." Rob sipped his beer, then explained, "It wasn't that I was being greedy when I accepted. I just thought that an extra hundred thousand would come in handy...pay off some bills. In my mind, I tried thinking of the flight as just another cargo run down to South America and back. I guess anything can be rationalized if a person has a reason for it. Anyway, the way I feel now, money doesn't mean shit. I'm glad as hell I'm finally out of the trade." Rob finished off his beer, then crushed the empty can with his fist. "Okay if I go grab myself another one?"

"Help yourself."

Rob limped over to the galley. "You about ready for a second one, too, Doug?"

"Please."

Rob pulled two Coors from the icebox and slowly worked his way back to the dinette. His ankle was throbbing with pain. He sat down and passed a beer across to Doug. "You know, I feel so relaxed talking to you. I've never been able to open up like this with anybody. Not even with Maureen. I mean, I told her things... personal things...but nothing like what we've talked about tonight."

"Talking can be a very effective mental medicine with the right listener."

"Yeah, well, thanks for listening. I owe you so much, Doug."

"You don't owe me anything."

A minute of silence was shared between the two men.

Then, suddenly, a serious expression spread across Rob's face. "Your wife said something Sunday night." He paused.

"Go ahead."

"It's about when she accused me of causing Susan's drug problem. That's not true. I never pushed drugs on the street...or anywhere. All I ever did was fly the stuff into the country for the organization. I swear. And if it hadn't been me, it would've been somebody else. There's thousands of hungry pilots out there willing to take the risk. I guess what I'm trying to get at is that it's not the pilot's fault for anybody's drug addiction. It's the users themselves. Just like in the days of Prohibition. The users are the ones who cause the demand. And as long as there's a demand, somebody's gonna smuggle it in...whether by plane or boat or however. Don't take me wrong. I'm not sticking up for smuggling or for drugs. What I did was illegal. But I never forced drugs down anybody's throat."

"But, Rob, smugglers *are* accomplices to the crime of drug addiction in a way."

"No, they aren't. All they're guilty of is bringing in an illegal substance. The people who do drugs...they're the ones who cause the drug abuse problem. And they're usually doing drugs because they *want* to do drugs. I can tell you that from personal experience."

"Personal experience? How personal?"

"I was once a user. I've been clean now for about seven years, but all the time I was on drugs, never once did one of my connections try to push anything on me. I bought *what* I wanted, *when* I wanted it...which was just about all the time."

"What you're telling me is that you chose to take drugs because you wanted to? You actually enjoyed it?"

"Yeah."

"Can I ask why?"

"'Cause it was the only way I could cope with my life at the time. It made me forget about my problems."

"But your problems are still with you."

"Yeah, they are...surprise."

"So what finally prompted you to quit?"

"You want the truth?"

Doug nodded.

"I scared the piss outta myself. That's the honest truth. I scared the fucking piss outta myself. One night I went over to this guy's house. It was him, me and his girlfriend. I'd already downed a couple of beers and when I got there, we smoked a mess of joints." It was all coming back to Rob, the memories of his drug-hazed days. "Then we popped quaaludes. I swallowed two." A chill ran through Rob's body as if the experience had happened only yesterday. "That was the killer...the double 'ludes. Once they kicked in, it was like I was glued to the carpet. I mean, I remember lying on the floor and not being able to move. Anyway, up until that night I'd never done the *lady*."

"Cocaine?"

"Yeah. I'd always been afraid of the stuff. But that night I was so low from the combination of beer, reefer and 'ludes, that I was ready to try anything...especially the *lady*. So I did three lines. Big lines." Rob swallowed unconsciously, then went on with his story. "Once the *coke* took effect I couldn't believe how great it was. I'd never felt anything open my mind like that cocaine high did. It just wound me up...recharged me. I never went to sleep that night. The three of us stayed up until dawn playing albums. Shit, I can still remember what we played...Led Zeppelin...Black Sabbath...Aerosmith." Rob chugged his beer, then confessed, "I never did drugs after that night."

Puzzled, Doug asked, "I can understand *why* you quit, but what actually *made* you quit? Just a few minutes ago you said you scared yourself into quitting. Now you're making it seem as if you really enjoyed the cocaine."

"This might sound stupid to you, Doug, but I *did* enjoy the *coke.* It was the best high I ever had on drugs. That's what scared me. I knew that if I continued doing drugs, cocaine would turn into a major dependency. Hell, I couldn't afford the stuff 'cause I was only making flight instructor's pay at the time. I started thinking about what I'd have to do to be able to buy it. I mean, that was long before I got involved with Falcon. But you know what the scariest part about that night was? It was when I realized how easily I could have overdosed from everything I had taken. So I just stopped. I quit...everything."

"I wish Susan could hear you say that. It might knock some sense into her."

"I'll tell her the whole story if you want me to."

"I'd appreciate that very much." Doug scratched an itch behind his ear. "It's all still very clear in your mind...the whole drug experience."

"Those kinds of things don't go away."

"I imagine they don't. You were fortunate to be able to quit cold-turkey like you did. Most people don't have the stamina."

"Yeah, I know. It didn't do much for my outlook on life, though."

"Leave that part out of the story when you talk to Susan, okay?"

"Yeah." Rob gulped down the last of his beer with one big swallow. "I hope you don't think I'm slime because of what I've told you tonight."

"I think you're honest for admitting your various involvements."

"Shit, Doug. You're so easy to talk to, you know? You don't automatically pass judgement." Rob stretched his arms behind his head. He liked Doug's style. He liked Doug. "Hey, Doug. Since I'm spilling my guts out like this—" He stopped, not sure if he should reveal any more of his past. But with the alcohol meandering through his bloodstream, taking control of him, loosening up his mind, Rob finally figured what the hell—go for it. Get it all out once and for all. He began slowly. "Doug, I...I wanna tell you about what happened to me eight years ago...what caused me to fall apart."

"I'm still listening."

Rob breathed deeply, then stated with remorse, "Her name was Rebecca." There, he said it. It was as simple as that. After eight long years of not saying her name aloud, he finally said it. He continued, "There wasn't anything I wouldn't have done for her...that's how much I loved her. Anyway, we shared this little apartment together in West Palm Beach. One night I came home after a late charter flight and Rebecca's car was parked in the driveway, but she wasn't home. I figured she was probably out with one of her girlfriends or something...which was okay with me. She did it all the time. She had a right to go out and have a good time when I was out flying. But later on, when I heard this car pull up in front of our apartment and she didn't come in, I went over to the front window and looked outside." Letting out eight years of anger, Rob cursed, "*That bitch* was giving head to some guy in the front seat of his car right there in front of our apartment." Rob was sweating heavily. He closed his eyes briefly, remembering the hurt he had felt. "I should've just gone outside and confronted her right then and there, but I didn't because I wanted to see what her excuse was going to be once she came inside. I mean, up until that night she'd always told me that she loved me...which I believed, but obviously it was a lie. Anyway, I waited until she finished up with him. I just sat there on the couch waiting for her to walk in through the doorway. And when she did...that's when I got the ultimate burn-job. She actually had the balls to tell me she was out dancing with her girlfriends. And then, when I asked her who the guy was in the car, she accused *me* of spying on *her*. I almost died right there. She tried making *me* feel like the guilty one. I left her the next morning and swore to myself never to get involved with anyone ever again." Rob closed his eyes, this time feeling emotionally released. He had gotten it out.

"Feel better?" Doug asked.

"I'm shaking and I don't know why."

"You should get some rest. You've been through a great deal of emotional stress on top of your physical injuries."

"Yeah, but I'm basically feeling good...just shaky. And I'm not tired." With his eyes still closed, Rob fell silent, his mind turning to deep thought. He thought about his new emotional freedom. He thought about where he was—on the sailboat. His shakes got worse. Suddenly, he realized why. He flashed open his eyes and looked pleadingly at Doug. Not wanting to lose his newly found freedom, he asked Doug, "What's gonna happen when we get back to Ft. Lauderdale?"

"You tell me, Rob."

"Damn, don't turn me in. Not after tonight."

"I thought we had this point settled?"

"We did, but that was before tonight. Please let me go, Doug." Rob was as serious as he could possibly be.

"Are you forgetting the conversation we had about me having every right to turn you over to the authorities?"

"I'm not forgetting. But I don't deserve to go to jail."

"Oh? Why not? You *were* involved in narcotics smuggling, weren't you?"

"Yeah, but I was forced into it...after the first run. And I've already suffered enough for that first mistake...emotionally and physically. Shit, I've been living in a walking prison ever since I got involved with Falcon. I know I did something wrong and I'm sorry for it. That's why I planned my escape from the organization...to get away from the hell of it all. I mean, it's not like I've planned a vacation or something. All I'm asking for from you is a second chance." Rob gazed upon Doug with begging eyes.

"Go on."

"I'm asking for a second chance at life because I know I can do better the second time around. I wanna go someplace where nobody knows me and I wanna start over."

"There's another side to this story, Rob."

"What's that?"

"Society likes to see its criminals incarcerated."

"But I'm not a criminal. Not really. I know that sounds stupid, but its true. I just...damn, I told you everything about me tonight. You should know that I've learned from my mistakes...that I've suffered."

"Sometimes that's not enough for society."

"In my case it is. Nobody will gain anything from having me locked away in a jail cell. And besides—" Rob was about to expand on his point when the drift of what Doug was saying burst into his head. He questioned Doug, "Why do you keep saying *society this* and *society that*?"

Doug smiled. "Let's just say that from everything I've heard tonight, I believe you. I just had to make sure that *you* believed you."

"Then this stuff about society wanting me put in

jail—"

Doug interrupted, "Each case has to be taken on its own merit, Rob. That's why our judicial system has a probationary sentence as an option."

"Are you gonna play judge and put me on probation?"

"Suppose I did. How would you suggest I sneak you past U.S. Customs? The stunt I'm pulling at Chub Cay won't work in Ft. Lauderdale."

"Well...I can take the Achilles in through the cut when *C'DOCKED'R*'s about a mile or two out from Port Everglades. That way, I won't be aboard the sailboat when you pull in to the Customs dock. And if you draw me a chart of the Ft. Lauderdale canal system, I can drop it off behind your house after dark. After that you'll never see or hear from me again. I'll somehow get across the state to Tampa."

"You have it all figured out, don't you?"

Rob didn't answer. He just looked at Doug with hope.

"I still can't give you a definite answer, Rob. This one's going to take a lot of thinking on my part. I have to think about my family, my professional life, my boat... many things. This is not a simple decision. If it makes you feel any better, though, I've always had a little renegade in my blood. But that's besides the point. Right now I have to get some sleep myself. I've got the midnight watch tonight." Doug stood up and walked back towards the after cabin. "Goodnight, Rob." He closed the door to the cabin.

Not being tired, Rob limped over to the companionway, grabbed hold of the wooden handrail and eased himself up the steps and into the cockpit, where he joined Susan and Maggie. Although his injured ankle was healing nicely, except for a constant throb, the climb up the companionway had not done him any good. Rob tried blocking the pain by sucking in a cool breath of night air until his lungs were filled to capacity. Then, slowly, he released the salty air, only to take in another breath. Several more times, Rob repeated his deep breathing cycle.

"You okay?" Susan asked with concern.

Rob nodded that he was while continuing to concentrate on ridding his ankle of pain.

Maggie wasn't so sure. "Go get your father, Susan," she insisted from her helmsman's position.

Rob reiterated, "No. I'm alright. My leg just hurts a little. That's all." He leaned back against the coaming and looked over toward Susan, who was staring back and directly into his eyes. When Susan lowered her gaze, Rob wondered what she was thinking. It didn't take long before he found out.

"Can I have your falcon charm?" she asked selfishly.

"You already asked me that and I said no."

"But that was before," Susan pouted. "Why can't I have it now?" She was acting like a ten year old whose parent wouldn't buy her the toy she wanted.

"Because," was the only word out of Rob's mouth. It was the only reason he could think of.

Susan still wasn't satisfied. "That's what you said last time, also. I don't understand why you want it."

Why *did* he still want it? Rob thought about that question real hard. Actually, it wasn't that he wanted the black falcon charm, but rather, something inside of him told him he still needed it. But after all he had revealed to Doug tonight, why would he still feel the need to possess the black bird-shaped stone? What power held him to the charm? Was it Falcon's will? Or was it something else—something stronger? But what could be stronger than Falcon?

Susan quickly changed the subject, asking Rob,

"Are you ever gonna see Maureen again?"

Maureen was the one thing Rob still did not want to talk about. Hiding his emotional hurt, he became defensive with his reply. "*She's* the one who walked out on me, so why should I want to go see her? It's obvious she doesn't want me anymore." It was only because of the letter he had sent to Maureen that Rob said what he said. In reality, he did want to see her, but he knew he couldn't.

Susan put forth, "I break up with my boyfriend all the time and we always get back together. I'll bet Maureen wants you back, too. It's a woman's right to change her mind."

"Maureen's different. She doesn't want me." Rob thought about what he had written in the letter, then said again, "She doesn't want me. Not now."

"You don't know that for sure." And with that said, Susan left the cockpit to get a cup of hot chocolate for herself from the galley.

For some odd reason, Susan's statement hit Rob with a powerful aftershock. He followed Susan down the companionway and pinned her against a locker in the galley. "Did you mean what you said up there?"

"What'd I say?"

"That Maureen might still want me?"

"I don't know, but she might. I would if I was her."

Rob confided in Susan, "Your dad might let me go free. He might let me take the Achilles when we get close to shore in Ft. Lauderdale. If he does, I was just wondering if maybe I should go see Maureen before heading over to Tampa? Maybe she'd go with me."

Rob had no way of knowing that Maggie had eavesdropped on his confession to Susan. He had no way of knowing what was going on inside Maggie's brain. He had no way of knowing that Maggie would have the final say on the matter.

CHAPTER TWENTY-FIVE

Thursday morning

On Wednesday, the sun had arisen fast and bright along the ocean's eastern horizon and had continued its daily trek across the Bahamian sky until it settled in the west at half past five. It had been a day that had slipped by quickly aboard *C'DOCKED'R,* almost as if the hours had passed into oblivion. Except for the Customs stopover at Chub Cay, which had gone down as smoothly as Doug had said it would—like silkwork—the day had been uneventful. The miles logged drew the sloop ever closer to its Florida landfall.

Thursday held greater anticipation as *C'DOCKED'R* sailed within sight of Ft. Lauderdale's condominium shoreline. With the Port Everglades channel positioned less than nine miles ahead, Doug was estimating a noon docking at the U.S. Customs station. After three and a half days of solid sailing, anxiety was building for what was to come.

Susan was at the helm of *C'DOCKED'R,* holding a steady course, keeping the boat lined up with the four red and white stripped smoke stacks belonging to Florida Power and Light's generating plant at Port Everglades. Doug and Rob were sitting on either side of Susan.

Maggie was the only member of the crew not on deck, for she had gone below to prepare lunch, the final meal of the cruise.

The horizon was hazy, but the azure sky above was gorgeous in color and filled with hundreds of tiny white clouds. The billowy cumulus were a godsend, bringing occasional bouts of coolness to the air as they shaded the sailboat.

Beyond the haze, to the south of Ft. Lauderdale's skyline, were the faint shadows of the pine trees lining the beach at John U. Lloyd State Park—one of the few natural beachfronts still remaining in South Florida.

With Thursday being a workday, the ocean practically belonged to *C'DOCKED'R*. A handful of party boats were drift-fishing along the reef, closer in to shore, probably loaded with tourists trying to play fishermen for the day. A few private charter boats trolled about in the deeper waters searching for marlin and other sport-fishing specimens. A single freighter crossed the horizon astern *C'DOCKED'R*, possibly on its way to the Caribbean. Besides those various vessels, *C'DOCKED'R* was alone off the Ft. Lauderdale coastline.

Had it been the weekend, the very same waters would have been teeming with literally hundreds of pleasure boaters, both power and sail—some fishing, others diving the reefs, and the rest just having a good time messing about in their boats. But today, the number of vessels could be counted on two hands.

With the wind dead astern and blowing lightly, *C'DOCKED'R* was running wing and wing, its mainsail vanged to starboard and its one-fifty genoa poled out to port. With each following wave, the sloop would surge forward, riding the wave's crest as if surfing. At least the boat's rolling motion wasn't too bad despite the shoal draft keel, though a much steadier ride would have been felt had *C'DOCKED'R* been full keeled—but then much of the Bahamas would have been ruled out as cruising ground for Doug and his family.

Maggie popped her head out of the hatchway. "Lunch is ready," she proclaimed cheerfully. As she climbed the companionway, she passed a tray of sandwiches out to Doug, then a pitcher of fruit punch and four plastic cups. Maggie took a seat next to her husband on the port side of the cockpit, across from Rob.

Doug held the tray out. "You'll enjoy these sandwiches," he told Rob. "Mag whips up an excellent tuna salad."

Rob reached for a sandwich, but then placed it back on the tray."

"What's the matter? Don't you like tuna?"

"Not with mayonnaise."

"That's how tuna's made," Maggie put forth. "The mayo adds texture."

"Yeah, but I eat it plain...or with mustard."

Doug cringed, "With mustard?"

"It's good."

Susan started laughing, then told her father, "Rob's a weird eater. He doesn't even like pizza or anything."

"Well, everyone has their own tastes, I guess." Doug said to Rob, "I'm sure you're hungry. Why don't you go down into the galley and open up a new can of tuna for yourself. Feel free to make it anyway you like."

"Thanks."

Maggie insisted, "Don't pour the oil down the drain. Use the glass jar in the sink."

"I don't drain the oil," Rob said, smiling as he got up and faced Maggie eye to eye. "It adds texture." Then, quick as a wink, he was down the companionway, out of Maggie's sight. He knew she hated him.

Maggie was furious. "Did you hear that snide remark he just made to me, Douglas? I'm telling you, he's been nothing but trouble right from the start."

"Calm down, Mag. Rob's not such a bad guy once you get to know him."

"He's a user, Douglas. A user of people. He used you. He used Susan. At least I had the fortitude to remain strong and do the right thing."

"Meaning what, Mag? What's the *right thing?*"

Maggie was hesitant. "Well, I...I wasn't going to tell you until we reached the bridge."

"Come on, Mag. I don't have time for guessing games. What are you up to?"

"When I was making the sandwiches, I..." Maggie paused for a few seconds, then blurted out, "I called the Coast Guard and told them about Rob."

"You did what?"

"I had to, Douglas. It was the right thing to do. Tuesday night, after you had gone to bed, I overheard Rob telling Susan how you were thinking about letting him take the Achilles and go free. I just couldn't sit back and let that happen. Too much has happened already that I disapprove of. I wasn't going to let you commit a criminal act on top of everything else you've done. I wasn't going to risk our marriage...our family. Rob is a drug smuggler, Douglas, and I'm going to make sure he goes to jail."

"Mag, if that's your only argument, then our own daughter should serve time also. Remember when she was arrested at school last year for possession of cocaine and drug paraphernalia? Or that time when she was caught shoplifting at the Galleria mall?"

"That's different."

"Not really. Only on a smaller scale. In fact, that was the original intent of this cruise, remember? We were going to give Susan a chance to start over...to start clean.

That's what Rob needs. A chance to wipe the slate clean. But now, because of what you've done, he won't get that chance." Doug leaned forward and called through the companionway hatch, "You'd better come up here, Rob. We've got a problem on our hands."

Rob climbed out into the cockpit and sat down across from Doug. "What's up?"

"Maggie called the Coast Guard. She told them about you."

Disbelief came to Rob, followed by the realization that he might as well have died in the crash, for now that the Coast Guard knew about him, it was only a matter of time before Falcon learned of his whereabouts. Rob stared blankly at Maggie. He couldn't help but think what an ugly person she was underneath her beautiful facial features. After all he had been through, after all he had survived, after all he had revealed to Doug, she had gone and done something so stupid—so deadly. It just wasn't fair. He coldly told Maggie, "Damn you...for signing our death warrants."

Rafael Ramairez stopped in front of the picture window in his office at the International Bank of Commerce. He leaned forward, resting his sturdy hands on the marble sill, looking out upon Biscayne Bay from so high a vantage point. The bay was all there for his mind to take in, for him to breath—its colors, its expansiveness. The bay was a beautiful sight to behold. A form of mental meditation. It was the only true peace in Rafael's violent world—Falcon's world.

Today had been an especially difficult day for Rafael at IBC. One of the bank's largest accounts, a Venezuelan-owned construction company, had been lost to another financial institution. The Venezuelan businessmen had transferred all of their assets to the competing bank with nary an explanation.

Fortunately for Rafael, he had an adept secretary who managed to swindle him an early afternoon appointment at the Chamber of Commerce building, giving him a handy excuse for breaking away from IBC earlier than usual. Today was a day for him to back off from the pressures of international finance.

The door to Rafael's penthouse office swung open, then closed with a slam. The well-tailored banker turned around to find Alec standing there alone. Rafael barked, "Why do you insist on barging in here like this. I'm in no mood to—"

"We've received word on Rob" Alec interrupted, knowing his intrusion would be forgiven once Rafael heard the news. "He's on a sailboat named *SEA DOCTOR*...spelled *C-D-O-C-K-E-D-R*. There's three other people aboard. A family from Ft. Lauderdale. They picked Rob up at Warderick Wells Cay. The boat's present bearing is zero-eight-seven degrees off the Port Everglades generating plant...approximately eight miles out right now. With the winds as light as they are, we've got about three hours to get a boat out to them before they reach the channel."

"Excellent!"

"Do you want all of them eliminated or just Rob?"

"Make sure Rob wears red. If the others happen to get caught up in the spray, it's no loss to us." Falcon gave no mercy—ever. He added, "I want my two top soldiers on this effort. And that new driver. The one who races in the offshore circuit. He knows the waters. Tell him I want the Cigarette pushed like his ass was on fire."

"The Cigarette's down in the Keys. No problem, though. I've got access to a Scarab docked over by Seventy-Ninth Street. It's thirty-eight feet of killer boat.

It flies, Rafael. It'll do seventy in open water."

"Do what you have to, Alec, as long as I get results. When I turn on the news tonight, I don't want to be disappointed." Before Falcon excused Alec from the privacy of his office, he added, "Russ finally came through for us."

"Not Russ," Alec corrected. "The information came from one of our boys over at U.S. Customs. The Coast Guard tipped them off about the sailboat."

Falcon turned his back on Alec and stared out the window. "Russ is a maggot to the organization. Take care of him for me, Alec." Falcon always got his way. His money saw to it that he did.

"Start the diesel," Doug instructed Susan. With his adrenalin now pumping in high gear and with a touch of nervousness thrown in, he was experiencing a slight personality change.

Susan did as she was told without reluctance or question. She fired up the diesel, shifted the Westerbeke into forward, then nudged the throttle halfway.

"Full throttle," Doug called out.

"Okay, daddy." More power was added. "Are you lowering the sails, daddy? Do you want me to head up into the wind so you can drop them?"

Doug glanced at the knotmeter. "No. We'll motorsail all the way to the cut. We need all the speed we can get right now." Doug then flippantly turned to his wife. "Exactly what did you tell the Coast Guard, Mag?"

Being rather vague with her answer, she replied, "Just that we're bringing in an injured smuggler who survived a plane crash in the Exumas. They seemed to know about the crash and asked why we had the pilot aboard. I told them you were a physician and that you felt it was the humane thing to do and that you've been treating his injuries since Sunday. I gave them our position, speed and course. They've instructed us to tie-up alongside the dock on Fifteenth Street, near where the Customs boats are kept. They said it's in front of a small white building next to the launch ramp. We're not suppose to use the regular Customs dock...the one we normally clear at."

"I know where this other one's at," Doug confirmed.

Rob broke into the conversation. "Look, all this talk's not doing us any damn bit of good. What we need out here is protection."

"Any suggestions?" Doug asked. "Because the only possible weapon I carry aboard *C'DOCKED'R* is a plastic emergency flare pistol."

With his mind working in record speed, Rob tried thinking up a way to protect himself and the Bakers from Falcon's retaliation. Then it came to him. "Can you patch me through to the Coast Guard on your VHF?"

"Mind if I ask what you're planning first?"

"I'm gonna try to save our asses," Rob replied calmly, feeling strong and secure about what he was going to do. He knew that the future of everyone aboard *C'DOCKED'R* depended upon the success of his radio call—and on the knowledge he held in his head about Falcon's organization. Rob explained, "I'm gonna tell the Coast Guard about the danger we're all in from Falcon. Then I'm gonna offer them a trade. In exchange for protection out here, I'll cooperate fully with the feds. I'll testify in court. There's a lot of stuff I know about the organization that I shouldn't have ever found out about. Insider-type stuff. I know things that'll help them bust Falcon and nail him to the wall. I know *who* Falcon is in real life. I wasn't suppose to know. Gustavo always acted as the middle man. But I found out accidentally. I'm sure they'd like to hear about it in court. And the worse that can happen to me for testifying against Falcon is that I'll end up dead...which is better than being killed out here with you all along with me. This way, you'll be safe. Who knows, at best maybe I'll get into the federal witness protection program."

"Then let's go make that call." Doug pointed to the companionway, followed Rob down into *C'DOCKED'R*'s main cabin and over to the navigation station. Doug took the seat by the radio, with Rob standing behind him.

Switching on the radio, Doug began broadcasting on VHF-FM channel 16. "This is the sloop *C'DOCKED'R*, calling Ft. Lauderdale Coast Guard."

An immediate response came over the speaker. "Sloop *C'DOCKED'R*, this is Ft. Lauderdale Coast Guard. We're aware of your situation, sir. Advise you switch to marine channel twenty-two."

"Switching to twenty-two," Doug said into the mike.

"Why do they want you to change frequencies?" Rob asked.

"Discreet channel." Doug rotated the channel selector knob clockwise. When the LED indicator light illuminated with the new frequency, he broadcasted, "The sloop *C'DOCKED'R* is on twenty-two."

"Sloop *C'DOCKED'R*, this is Ft. Lauderdale Coast Guard. Go ahead, sir."

"Stand by," Doug told the Coast Guardsman as he rose from his seat and pointed for Rob to take his place. He handed the mike to Rob. "It's all yours. Good luck."

Thirty-two minutes after Alec had placed a single telephone call, two Colombian gunmen and an American driver were racing away from the 79th Street yacht basin in their borrowed thirty-eight footer—a candy-apple red Scarab. Goggles protected their eyes from the tearing force of the speed-induced wind. Both throttles were held wide open by the driver, as the three men leaned against stand-up bolsters.

A pair of silvery rooster tails streamed brilliantly behind the Scarab as the V-hulled powerboat traveled the glassy green waters of upper Biscayne Bay, on its way towards Government Cut and the ocean. The rooster tails gave the boat a fierce appearance as it practically skimmed the bay's watery surface.

When the Scarab came upon a *NO WAKE* zone, thoughts of throttling down never even entered the driver's mind. His realm *was* the world of speed—watery speed. Besides, the powerful Scarab could easily out-run the meager boats operated by Metro-Dade's Marine Patrol.

Again, no concern was shown by the Scarab's experienced driver as he barreled the boat underneath a minimal clearance bascule bridge. In fact, Falcon's driver wasn't phased in the least.

Then, as he made a sharp turn to the east, leading him into Government Cut, he saw a huge twin-engined seaplane making its final approach for a water landing in the channel. The descent path of the Grumman Mallard put the plane on a collision course with the Scarab, causing the boat's driver to feel challenged to a game of chicken. Not only did Falcon's driver have iron guts, he also had stainless-steel balls.

He held fast to his course, despite the aircraft's right-of-way. He knew he'd win. He was right, too, as the pilot of the turbine-powered Grumman executed a missed approach, gaining altitude overhead before turning back for a second landing attempt. Elation overcame the Scarab's driver and he laughed excessively, all the while heading the V-hull down the channel towards the open Atlantic Ocean.

It wasn't long before he was driving the bright red Scarab through the waves about four miles offshore of Hollywood Beach. When he came abeam the Dania Fishing Pier, the two Colombian hitmen signaled him to back off on the throttles and stop the boat dead in the water. He didn't argue. Both Colombians were brandishing AR-15 machine guns armed with full clips.

The Colombian nearest to the driver, using his weapon as a pointer, outstretched his right arm in the direction of a Coast Guard helicopter approximately three miles ahead of the Scarab. The Sikorsky, normally used for search and rescue missions by the Coast Guard, was hovering about five hundred feet above and behind a single-masted sailboat. It was the only sailboat in sight. This led the Colombian national to one conclusion. *"Ahi esta el barco! Lo llaman el doctor del mar! Ese es el barco que vamos a disparar!"* he shouted with adrenalin-heightened anticipation. *"Vamos a hundir esos hifueputas!"* A successful ocean rendevous had been made. *C'DOCKED'R* was within sight.

Although the American driver spoke very little Spanish, he understood the meaning behind the Colombian's excitement—something about wasting the sonova-bitches. All that remained now was for him to bring the Scarab close enough to the sailboat for Falcon's two gunmen to make their hit. And screw the goddamned chopper, he thought with much bravado. As far as he was concerned, the presence of the helicopter posed no threat to him whatsoever. Nor did he foresee any problems arising from a drift-fishing boat about a quarter of a mile off the sailboat's starboard bow. He'd been in tighter situations before.

As soon as the Colombians gave the go-ahead, the

driver began his high-speed approach towards *C'DOCKED'R*. Within two minutes, only a mile and a half of ocean separated the Scarab from the sailboat as the driver closed the gap on his target. The distance between the boats grew less as each second became history. Soon there was but half a mile of separation. Then three-eighths of a mile. The driver thought it strange that the chopper did not move from its hovering position. Surely the chopper crew saw the Scarab racing towards the sailboat, he assumed.

When only an eighth of a mile remained between the Scarab and *C'DOCKED'R*, it became apparent to the driver that nobody was in the sailboat's cockpit. He figured the people aboard the sailboat must have spotted the Scarab and realizing what was about to happen, scurried below to hide in the cabin. He laughed as he drew the Scarab even closer to the sailboat, for he knew the fiberglass hull of *C'DOCKED'R* was no match for the high-velocity bullets of the AR-15's.

At first, the Scarab's driver saw it only as a lightning-fast blur that came whipping around from the far side of the drift-fishing vessel. But then, when it came at him with blinding speed from the port side, he was forced to swing hard around to starboard and away from the sailboat in order to escape whatever it was that was chasing him.

The Scarab's turn had put *C'DOCKED'R* out of firing range of Falcon's two gunmen. Realizing this, the driver tried dangerously to work his way back toward the sailboat. As he made an evasive series of radical S-turns, a quick glance over his shoulder revealed the truth to him—he was being chased by a U.S. Customs drug interception boat.

The Customs boat, an ex-doper Cigarette confiscated in a drug bust, was barreling down upon the

Scarab's high flying rooster tails with alarming speed, despite its being strapped with slightly less horsepower. Falcon's cocky driver, being the professional offshore racer that he was, possessed the reflexes of an alley cat when it came to boat handling. After out-maneuvering the thirty-one foot Cigarette, he managed to bring the Scarab close enough to *C'DOCKED'R* to allow the gunmen to empty their entire clips into the sailboat's hull, splattering the fiberglass with dozens of holes. The crew inside the sailboat were unquestionably either dead or seriously incapacitated by the attack, the driver thought.

Just to be positive, though, he chose to bring the Scarab around for one final run, all the while eluding the Cigarette. The gunmen, with fresh clips in their AR-15's, once again fired at the helpless sailboat. This time, however, they were being fired upon themselves by the agents aboard the Customs boat. One of Falcon's gunmen was hit and killed instantly. He slumped over, his blood spraying the boat's cockpit. The second gunman reloaded with a new clip, turned around and let his AR-15 rip into the Customs boat.

The driver of the Scarab now had to make a quick decision. Should he head back to Government Cut via the open water of the ocean or were his chances of survival better if he made a fast sprint into Port Everglades and then out-maneuver the Cigarette on Ft. Lauderdale's intricate Venice-like canal system? Immediately, he broke off the attack on the sailboat and aimed for Port Everglades.

Although he raced the Scarab at top speed towards the red and green markers of the entrance channel, the three minute ride seemed to stretch into an eternity. When he finally drove the boat between the rocky breakwaters of the harbor's entrance, a momentary sigh of relief escaped from deep within his sweat-soaked body, for he'd managed to stay well enough ahead of the Cigarette to avoid being shot at by the pursuing Customs agents.

Once inside the harbor's turning basin, the driver swung the Scarab ninety degrees to starboard and headed straight for the 17th Street Causeway, passing beneath the bridge at an excessive rate of speed. The wake from his boat strained the docklines of the million dollar yachts tied up alongside the nearby marinas.

He sped past markers 27, 25, 23 and 21 of the Intracoastal Waterway system and then, in his quest to gain even more distance on the Customs boat, just narrowly missed hitting the piling of channel marker 19 as he rounded a bend to the right.

With a hotel and marina lying a quarter of a mile dead ahead, the Scarab's driver had to make another quick decision—this time, whether to turn left or right. He knew that Lake Sylvia was off to the right and that several canals branched out from the lake's perimeter. But it had been many years since he'd last anchored overnight in Lake Sylvia and he couldn't recall what the critical clearances were for the low-level bridges which spanned the canals.

Rather than trap himself without an exit, he chose to play it safe for a change. Turning left, he continued along the Intracoastal Waterway in a northerly direction, aiming for the Las Olas Boulevard bridge. An Olympic-size swimming pool and diving center off to the right was nothing but a blurry vision out the corner of his eyes as he thundered past on his way toward the bridge.

Wondering how far back the Cigarette was, he decided to catch a glance of the Customs boat. In the short instant it took him to turn his head around, his life had ended, as did the life of Falcon's second gunman.

Somehow, the Cigarette had gained on Falcon's

driver and, when a single shot fired from the high-powered rifle of a Customs agent found its way into the fuel tank of the Scarab, the boat ignited, sending skyward a billowing orange ball of flame.

A secondary explosion erupted when the Scarab's fiery carcass slammed head-on into a concrete seawall, hurtling splintered pieces of fiberglass and metal through the air. Within minutes, the burning remains of the Scarab sank to the muddy bottom of the Intracoastal Waterway.

C'DOCKED'R was still sailing on course towards the Port Everglades channel as if the attack had never taken place—such was the reliability of the sloop's autohelm. Down below, all was quiet, except for the sound of seawater running in through dozens of holes on the hull's port side. Overall, however, damage was minimal. *C'DOCKED'R* was repairable.

C'DOCKED'R's crew had faired even better than the boat, for they had witnessed the assault from the safety of the Sikorsky's belly. It had been Rob's last minute brainstorm to have the four of them airlifted into the helicopter. The plan had gone off without a hitch. They had survived the ordeal. They had survived Falcon.

With word that the Scarab had exploded, one of the helicopter's aircrewmen helped Doug into the safety basket and slowly lowered him by cable down into *C'DOCKED'R*'s cockpit. Susan, Maggie and Rob were then lowered in turn.

Sitting behind the wheel, Doug disengaged the autohelm, once again establishing manual control of his sloop. A few minutes later, a forty-one foot Coast Guard UTB boat came out to meet *C'DOCKED'R*, providing a much welcome escort service for the final run into port.

It felt good to be alive. It felt good to be home.

EPILOGUE

Thursday evening
    C'DOCKED'R had been tied up to the Fifteenth Street dock since quarter past one in the afternoon, but it wasn't until after five o'clock that Rob was granted a breather from preliminary questioning by the DEA. Handcuffed to the wrist of a Federal marshal, Rob left the white building, walking slowly due to his sea legs. Twice he had to grab onto the marshal's arm because of his unsteady balance.
    Carefully trying not to apply too much pressure to his bad ankle, Rob limped toward the dock, taking great pleasure in the light breeze caressing his face as he walked past the building. It was such a simple joy to feel the coolness, yet one filled with new splendor. Rob knew his life was finally beginning to come together and he liked what he saw. Most of all, he liked himself.
    At the dock, Rob was glad to see Doug, who was still aboard *C'DOCKED'R*, fiddling around on deck. Neither of them had had a chance to say good-bye to each other. Rob stepped down into the sailboat's cockpit, the Federal marshal tagging along like a shadow. Rob turned to the government man. "Any chance of me talking to my friend here alone?"

The marshal obliged Rob's inquiry by releasing his own wrist from the handcuff and relocking the metal device to *C'DOCKED'R*'s sturdy teak handrail. Then, backing off the boat and down the dock, he gave Rob thirty feet of freedom, all the while his fingers never leaving the grip of a .357 Magnum holstered to his waist.

Not knowing quite what to say, Rob just stared across the boat at Doug, who was busy coiling a line on the foredeck.

Doug looked up. Sensing Rob's uneasiness, he decided to break the ice. Nodding his head toward the white building, he asked, "How're things going in there?"

"Okay, I guess. They seem to like the information I'm giving them. They're taping everything and writing pages of notes. I've been offered witness protection."

"I'm glad to hear that, Rob. I'm also glad to see they're treating you decently in there. You look good... cheerful."

"The feds aren't roughing me up or anything, if that's what you mean."

"That's exactly what I mean."

Rob took a peek down into the sailboat's main cabin. "Where's your family?"

"Maggie and Susan went home a few hours ago."

"Oh."

"Susan wishes you all the best. She also wanted me to ask you if she can have your bird charm. I promised her I'd ask."

Rob reached into his shirt. Clutching the falcon charm, he jerked swiftly, breaking the finely crafted piece of jewelry from its chain. He held it out for Doug to see. "This black falcon stands for pain and death. It's not something I'd wanna give away as a reminder of me."

"I understand."

"I hope Susan will, too," Rob stressed, as he stuffed

the charm into the pocket of his borrowed pants.

"I'm sure she will...after a while." Doug cleared his throat. "Rob...I want to thank you for that chat you had with Susan about your experiences with drug abuse. It's worth more coming from someone who's been there."

"I don't know if it really did any good, though. She didn't seem to show any emotion or concern over it."

"Time will tell, Rob. The important thing is you told her."

When the two men broke into a momentary silence, the only sound heard was the constant stream of water being pumped overboard by *C'DOCKED'R*'s bilge pump.

"Sorry about your boat," Rob apologized. "I feel responsible."

"Well, don't. That's why I carry insurance. Besides, I've been thinking about trading up soon. This gives me an excuse to do it now. After repairs are made, I'll probably trade *C'DOCKED'R* in for something in the fortyish range."

"Forty thousand dollars?"

Doug laughed. "No forty feet...or thereabouts. And you can add a good hundred thousand to your cost estimate. It's time old Douglas Baker put himself in hock... just for the fun of it, of course."

"What'd you mean by that?"

"Believe it or not, Rob, you've taught me something very valuable on this cruise."

"Yeah? What's that?"

"How fragile life is. How each day *must*...and I emphasize the word *must*...be lived to its fullest. There's no room for compromise."

Rob wore a puzzled expression.

"You don't have any idea what I'm talking about, do you?"

"Not really. You started saying something about buying a new boat. After that, you lost me."

"Rob, I've had this one particular dream for most of my life...to circumnavigate the globe on a sailboat...a wooden sailboat with baggywrinkles and bowsprit. I want to anchor in exotic ports-of-call, meet people of different cultures, taste unusual foods." Doug went on, "This afternoon, Rob, if it hadn't been for that Coast Guard helicopter airlifting us aboard, I would've lost the chance to ever fulfill my dream. I'm not willing to risk losing that chance again. So...I've made a decision. I'm giving up my medical practice to go for my dream."

"That's kind of a big deal to decide all of a sudden... without thinking it over, I mean. What about your wife? And Susan?"

"You don't have to feel guilty, Rob. Mag's known about the dream for as long as we've been married. She's always known that the time would come someday. When I tell her that *someday* has arrived, she'll understand. And Susan can finish high school through correspondence classes. Lot's of cruising kids do it. As for your comment about not having thought it over...I've thought it over plenty...ever since I was a little boy."

"Oh."

"I've thought about transiting the Panama Canal and sailing the Coconut Milk Run down to Tahiti. I've thought about hammocking in the shade of rustling palm trees. I've even considered taking a delve off the beaten path and heading over to Rarotonga in the Cook Islands. Not many people cruise there."

Doug threw a glassy-eyed stare over *C'DOCKED'R*'s port rail, gazing down at the murky water. "I've even picked out a name for the boat...*ANCIENT WINGS*. It's the perfect name for a wooden boat." Doug recast his dreamy eyes upon Rob. "There's this place down in the

British Virgin Islands...on the western shore of Tortola... Cane Garden Bay. If I died there, I'd know I'd died in heaven. It's absolute paradise. Picture in your mind a white cresent-shaped beach lined from end to end with lush coconut palms and a tire swing hanging down from one of the those trees. Imagine gentle waves lapping onto the powdery sand at the water's edge. Imagine too, vegetation-covered mountains rising majestically all around, up toward a clear blue sky, with tradewind breezes dancing down from the mountains and onto the bay and the smell of the sea filling the air day and night. Best of all, though, there's this little establishment right there on the beach. A guy can go there and grab a cheeseburger, listen to a steel drum band and sip the best darn margaritas anywhere in the Caribbean. I know because I've been there many times."

The Federal marshal was beginning to show signs of itchy feet and nervousness. He moved closer to the sailboat, then right up next to it. Upon hearing talk of the Caribbean Sea, he boarded *C'DOCKED'R* and rehandcuffed himself to Rob. "Alright, hot-shot," he grimaced at Rob. "You've had long enough. Finish up what you have to say and then let's get going."

"I was supposed to get half an hour," Rob argued.

"I said let's go!"

Rob motioned for Doug to come back to the cockpit. When he did, Rob embraced him in a one-armed hug of friendship. "I'll never forget what you've done for me, Doug. This whole experience...this past week..." Rob couldn't get the words out. "Say good-bye to Susan for me. And good luck with your wooden boat. I hope you find what you're after. Take care." Tears filled Rob's eyes as he stepped off the boat with the marshal, leaving Doug alone in *C'DOCKED'R*'s cockpit.

"You have a peaceful life yourself, Rob," Doug

shouted out, realizing he'd never see Rob again. They were two lives on diverging paths that had crossed to share an awakening experience.

As Rob was led up the walk, he made an eye-sweep of the area and spotted a phone booth over by the boat launch ramp. He stopped the marshal. "Before we go back inside, can I make a quick call on that phone over there?"

"Only if it's brief."

"I said a quick call."

The government man escorted Rob over to the pay phone.

"Got a quarter?" Rob asked.

"You're something else," the marshal expressed with sarcasm, as he reached into his pocket for change. He pulled out a quarter and placed it on the small metal shelf inside the booth.

Meantime, Rob searched the yellow pages for the listing he needed. When he couldn't find it, he slammed the book closed. "Shit!" he vented after realizing he'd been flipping through the Ft. Lauderdale edition of the telephone directory. Wasting the marshal's quarter on a call to Information, Rob said, "Miami Springs," when the girl asked him what city he wanted. He then told her whose number he was looking for and memorized the girl's reply. Memory came easy for Rob. Copying IFR clearances over the years had been good for something. He turned back to the marshal once again. "The call's long distance from here. You got any more change?"

Begrudgingly, the marshal emptied his pocket, giving Rob every coin he had, including the pennies.

Rob dropped another quarter into the slot, waited for the tone, dialed 1 and then the number. An operator came on the line and instructed him on how much additional coinage he needed to place the call, which he deposited. Rob then handed the rest of the coins back to the marshal, including the pennies. Several rings went by before an unfamiliar female voice answered at the other end of the phoneline. Rob was nervous. He hated telephones. "Um, is Jackie there? Or Maureen?"

"Well, which one do you want? They're both here," the girl said rudely.

"Um, um, Maureen." Rob hated phones—something that went back many years.

"Hold on. I'll go get her."

Rob heard the phone being carelessly dropped onto the bar counter at the *Flight Deck Lounge*. After about a twenty second silence, it was again picked up.

"Hello, this is Maureen. Can I help you?"

"Maureen, it's me."

"Rob? Where are you? I thought—"

"I'm okay. I'm up in Ft. Lauderdale under federal custody. I'm gonna be a witness for them against Falcon."

"But your letter said—"

"Forget the letter. I've changed since then, Maureen. Look, I don't have much time to talk right now, so I can't really explain anything." Rob swallowed hard before going on. "Maureen...I love you!" He waited for her to hang up on him.

"I love you, too, Rob."

"You do?" He was surprised—Susan had been right.

"Yes, I do. Very much."

Finally able to face his true feelings, Rob said into the phone, "I want you to be my wife, Maureen. I want you to come with me to wherever it is they send me in the witness protection program."

Maureen shouted an immediate, "*Yes!* Oh, yes, Rob. I will marry you." Two long years of waiting, praying and hoping were over. She'd gotten the man she wanted—the man she loved. Rob wanted to talk longer, but he knew his time was running short. He bid Maureen a temporary good-bye, clicked the receiver back onto its hook and stepped out of the booth and over to the seawall. Still handcuffed to the marshal's wrist, Rob awkwardly reached into his pocket and pulled out the black falcon charm. His mysterious inner need to possess it was gone.

Switching the falcon to his right hand—the one with the heavy fiberglass cast on it—Rob heaved the charm into the air, watching as the custom-made piece of jewelry arched upward, then down, until finally it struck the watery surface of the canal and sank. A series of circular ripples were all that remained of the black falcon.

THE END

Have your ever wanted to write and publish your own book?
Chevy Alden teaches you how in his award-winning manual:

"How To Get Published - Guaranteed"

Complete details about this book can be found on the next page.

ATTENTION: AVIATION & NAUTICAL GROUPS

Is your organization looking for a highly-motivated guest speaker to tell your members how they can write and publish their own air-sea books? Award-winning author Chevy Alden makes year-round guest appearances at aviation and nautical-related trade shows, conferences and association meetings. For detailed information, please write to: Alden Speaking Engagements, c/o Tri-Pacer Press, P. O. Box 840111, Pembroke Pines, Florida, 33084-2111.

"How To Get Published - Guaranteed"

by Chevy Alden

Written in an easy-to-read narrative format, this 328-page self-help manual describes the publishing process from an insiders point-of-view. Topics include writing, editing, publishing, promotion and marketing. Alden's finely-crafted text is enriched with more than 100 photos, illustrations, documents, publishing forms and sample letters. This book received an *NAIP Special Publishing Award* from the National Association of Independent Publishers and is sure to become a classic. A real bargain at $18.95 plus shipping.

Here are a few of the reviews this book has received:

"People who use Alden's manual are on their way to a successful career as a published author."
--Henry Holden, Black Hawk Publishing

"We are adding this book to our reference collection. It will be a very useful addition to the Center."
--Karin Taylor, Small Press Reference Center

"Alden has an easily understood style that assists the reader in grasping the fantastic world of publishing."
--Betsy Lampe, Book Review Editor, NAIP

"Written with clarity, directness, logic, and a positive attitude...a winner."
--George Diamond, Ph.D., English Department, Moravian College

"An important guide."
--Robert Milne, Editor, Travelwriter Marketletter

To order your copy, send $18.95 plus $2.00 for shipping. (Check or Money Order only)

Mail your order to: Tri-Pacer Press
　　　　　　　　　　 P.O. Box 840111-BF
Florida residents
add 6% sales tax   Pembroke Pines, FL 33084-2111